HERE COMES THE SUN

THE HARDEST THING ABOUT MIDDLE AGE IS GROWING OUT OF IT

FAWN GERMER

To Cathy,

Don't wait. Do it NOW!

Fawn
2025

YOLO — you only live once

First published in the United States by Boulevard Books, an imprint of Newhouse
Publishing

Here Comes the Sun. Copyright © 2025 by Fawn Germer. All rights reserved. Printed in
the United States of America.

Printed in the United States of America

Hardcover ISBN 978-0-9838772-9-5
Paperback Color ISBN 978-0-9795466-5-5
Paperback Black and White ISBN 978-0-9795466-7-9
E-book ISBN 978-0-9838772-7-1

All rights reserved. No part of this book may be reproduced in any form or by any
electronic or mechanical means without permission in writing from the publisher or
author, except by a reviewer, who may quote brief passages in a review.

www.fawngermer.com

Speaking information: info@fawngermer.com (727) 467-0202

To Sonny, my significant other.

INTRODUCTION

I did not climb Mount Everest, hike the Pacific Crest Trail, or eat, pray, and love my way around the world. All I did was go for a really long ride with my dog.

People do that all the time. It doesn't seem special; you can't say it was extraordinary.

But it was.

I woke up one day, feeling suddenly old. My friends were dying young, my career was in a slump, and my life was not fixing itself. Dismissed, invisible, wrinkled, and vulnerable—I felt all of that, like my best years were behind me and time was running out.

It was a rare dark storyline in an exceedingly happy life.

By all appearances, my life was fabulous. The world I shared via social media was one of endless beach walks, camping under the stars, and kayaking adventures under a full moon, at sunrise or sunset.

I *was* living an amazing life.

But, as my friends started getting sick and dying at way-too-young ages, I had to confront something: I'm not going to live forever, and I can no longer deceive myself that I am middle-aged.

How many years do I have left? Twenty? Thirty? Forty? Am I spending my time right? My mom was paralyzed by a stroke when she was 66 and was sick for 22 years until she died. Was she betrayed by heredity or fate? I started wondering when fate would turn on me because fate turns on all of us at some point.

How much time do I have?

I've always wanted to hit the road in an RV after I retired, but I wasn't retired—just restless. And a bit lost. I needed a reset. I wanted my spark back.

So I ran away from home with my dog.

I needed to challenge everything that made me feel weak on the inside. Age, wrinkles, my career, the instability of our country and the world. The common anger and nastiness in people I encountered in everyday life and the anger I was seeing in people driving on US 19. That was for starters.

I was worn out trying to figure out who I was at 62. I needed to just *be* who I was.

I bought a van and planned to live the adventure of a lifetime.

It scared the hell out of me.

What if I get lost? I could have a heart attack. Should I bring a gun? I should bring a gun. I don't want a gun. What am I doing? What if I fall while hiking? My van could break down in the middle of nowhere. What if something happens to Sonny? I could be in the hospital unconscious with nobody to make decisions for me. I could get killed. Raped.

Nobody will even know where I am.

I will not be safe.

Fear taunted me, filling me with doubt and tempting me to give up on my dream. I'm sure part of it was that the trip would change my life —and my life needed changing.

The what-ifs were so loud, and they were getting louder. My biggest challenge wasn't loading up my dog and driving across the country to find myself. It was getting out of the driveway.

After the stress of packing, getting my will notarized and my home in order, delivering my two cats to my friend Jane, and saying goodbye to my loved ones, I called Sonny to the van, chose a 1980s playlist on Spotify, turned the key in the ignition, and took off.

The minute I left, I was fine. *Free.* Instantly. No schedule, no doomsday news from the internet, no worrying about expectations of others, no mail, no chores, no home repairs, no work, no Zoom meetings, and, for the first time ever, no plan.

Freedom.

In that van, I was my own country. I decided what energy to let into my life, positive or negative. I controlled my consumption of the news and my encounters with others. I would get up, adventure with Sonny, come and go when I felt like it, move or stop at a whim, and go to bed whenever.

And yet, every time I felt I had escaped, I got another sad reminder of the reality we can never elude. In four months, I lost friends who were 58, 59, 63 64, 67, and 70. I lost two more when I returned, ages 59 and 63.

None of them knew it was coming.

This is the seventh draft of this book because I kept hiding that sad reality. I didn't want to talk about all that loss because I didn't want to depress you. But I came to realize that the hard, heartbreaking lessons of death have actually led me to an awakening that will give me a much happier life.

If the clock is ticking louder and things can change in an instant, we'd better get moving and bet on today.

I now live by the mantra: "Don't wait. Don't wait. Don't wait."

My friend Patty Ivey saw my "Don't wait" video on Facebook as she got word her friend, Sylvie, had Stage 4 lung cancer. Friends were planning to drive from all over Florida to see her, but the timing was terrible for Patty, whose schedule was jammed.

"But I wanted to support my friend," she said. "I kept thinking, 'Don't wait.'" She canceled everything and went. A dozen girlfriends convened with Sylvie, reminiscing, joking, and wrapping her with love.

Three days later, Sylvie was gone. She was 62.

This moment—right here, right now—*this* is your life. You do not know what is coming.

You *can't* wait. Life is getting harder. There will be more tears, not fewer.

Do what you need to do. Go where you want to go. Call people, see people, say what you need to say. Stop arguing and make peace.

Time is running out.

When I was driving in my van, I would dictate my thoughts and, at night, I'd add everything to my journal and write. My greatest joy wasn't hiking, cycling, kayaking, seeing people, or photographing scenery. It was opening my laptop and writing every night, with my little buddy at my side. It was taking pictures with my iPhone and posting them every morning. I hoped my photography and writing would add up to some sort of a book, but I didn't know how scared I would be to share what I was writing. I feel exposed, revealing so much (or too much) of my truth. This feels vulnerable.

But I grew. Wow. I did grow.

I feel an even louder call to hike the mountains, enjoy my friends, embrace the sky, and laugh every day, filling every breath with life, not loss. When waves of sadness came over me this summer, I stopped myself, looked around, then felt gratitude.

I am alive. I will not wait, I will not wait, I will not wait.

PART 1: SOMETHING'S GOTTA GIVE

MIDDLE-AGED+

The light is good, but really, it's bad because I can see everything. Every single line on my face. All of them. *Who is that? How did that middle-aged woman break into my mirror? Where did I go, because that reflection I see is definitely not me. She's so ... so ... so mature! Bull. She's old. Middle-aged nothing. Lines around the eyes, around the mouth, smile lines, frown lines, crow's feet, worry lines ...*

Hey!

Hey!

How did this happen?

The first time I noticed the wrinkles, I was riding in a shuttle to the airport. The light was bright as I looked at my reflection in the big rearview mirror. There was no hiding the age in my face, and it upset me because I was only 40.

I looked older than that. It kinda geeked me out, so I called my best friend Joyce—she's 11 years older than me—on my cell phone and told her what I was experiencing.

"Oh, that's happened to me many times," she said in a comforting voice. "The one thing I have to tell you is: It gets worse."

What was weird was that I looked old but didn't feel old at all. I don't even feel 40 now, and I'm in my sixties. On the inside, I'm between 28 and 34, depending on the day.

But I look at that reflection now and wonder how all of this happened so fast. Time races by, and it's moving faster every year. We either age or we die, and I am not in a hurry to die.

If I have to face aging, I'm going to do it on my own terms. I'm not going to whimper my way through this, lamenting all that I am not. My plan is to work with what I have because I have a lot.

I feel young and powerful, except when I see my reflection in the mirror or, worse, in the eyes of younger people who think of me as their grandmother's age. Or when a store clerk asks me if I'm retired. (Oh yes, she did, and oh no, I am not.) Or when young people don't talk to me on airplanes.

I'm at my professional best, my personal wisest. I feel fan-freakin'-tastic. And yet, it's as if I am invisible.

I am roaring on the inside, but time has turned my volume down on the outside.

I have to do something.

I am having an identity crisis. My career is having an identity crisis. I don't even know how to write this, because it feels like I'm revealing too much, especially after everything I have said and stood for as a corporate motivational speaker and author for more than two decades. But this is eating at me. It has been eating at me for a couple of years.

Here goes:

I am sick of talking about how to lead and succeed in the corporate world. Something has happened inside of me and, frankly, I don't care one whit. Not in the slightest.

Saying this is like Santa confessing that he's over Christmas. But I've said everything I need to say about leadership strategies and career success. I wrote a shelf full of books on it. What else is there to say? I already said it.

So I'm not doing it. And since I'm not doing it, I have to take stock of what I *am* doing, and frankly, what I am doing is floundering.

I have to do something. I'm not sure what.

I have to do *something*.

I'm not worried about my mortality. I have always been at peace with it. But I do ponder my time. How do I want to use the time I have to live the best life possible? I've always filled my spare time with adventure, but I want more. I'm healthy and want to squeeze every bit of life out of every single minute.

I can't continue to con myself into believing I am middle-aged. But I don't see myself as a senior citizen, either, especially since, as I said, it feels on the inside like I'm somewhere between 28 and 34. I have invented the term, "Middle-aged Plus" for where I am chronologically, but it does feel like I am on the other side of something.

I have lost something momentarily, and I think what I've lost is my confidence. I hate that I feel that way, and it's embarrassing for a motivational speaker to feel that way, but I want to be honest. I'm willing to put that in writing because I know that my strong self is still inside, and I refuse to give in to a weaker self. I'm certain I am a short way away from finding the bold me, but that isn't going to happen at my desk in Florida, waiting for everything to magically come together.

I think about that, but I am equally struggling with what has happened to our society. People are angry, politics are ripping us apart, we hear disturbing talk of racism, antisemitism, guns, gender, nukes, war, inflation, power grabs—and all of that negativity and hatred is overwhelming, even to an eternal optimist like me. And I AM an eternal optimist. But I need to go hang out in the woods for a while and tune out the chaos.

That's it. People are always doing cleanses and detoxes. I want to detox from the ugly. I want to meet people and not wonder whether they are a Democrat or Republican or if they are angry or whether they are carrying a gun. I want to smell fresh air and not think about tomorrow or yesterday.

My mom's stroke happened at age 66, and it paralyzed her for the last twenty-two years of her life. She was four years older than I am now. I was 31 at the time, and my perception was that, at 66, she was old. I thought what happened to her was what happened to older people. The Alzheimer's disease showed up about ten years after the stroke, so her ordeal was monumental. I now realize how young she was.

After her stroke, I made up my mind to do something every day to make today different from yesterday. I wanted every day to matter, and so I stopped defining myself by my work. Work is important! It has always mattered to me. But it has never been who I am. It has been what I do. The choice to live that way has let me lead a joyful life, despite its inevitable challenges. There was always a choice between work and life, and I always chose life.

The sun rises and sets everywhere, and it is beautiful. I always find magic there.

People tell me they wish they had my life. Several have said my posts on social media chronicling my adventures have depressed them because their life isn't as interesting.

That is upsetting. Ninety percent of what I do costs nothing except effort, so I have always lived large. But something is off. I feel the need to do something radical.

I have to do something dramatic.

I need to get out of Florida.

MY $10 DOG

Four years ago, I brought home a black and white pittie named Brutus from Manatee County Animal Services. He was a year old and had been in three shelters.

One of the staffers asked what I was looking for. I described Louie, my most perfect dog who had died almost two years earlier.

"I would like a well-behaved, laid-back, quiet dog," I said. "Preferably a black-and-white pit bull."

"That's your dog," she said, pointing at Brutus.

I hadn't noticed him! I took him out to the play yard, and he ran like he'd finally been set free after being imprisoned for years. He wouldn't stop. He wasn't selling himself as the quiet dog I was looking for, but I knew he was probably nervous and desperate to get out of that smelly, loud kennel. I trusted the lady in the shelter and brought him home to see if he would get along with my cats.

I fell in love with him, and he demurred when the cats showed him who was boss. I went back the next day to formalize the adoption.

"You are in luck," the lady said. "He just went on sale for $10."

All this for less than the cost of a pizza.

"Brutus" is the name of the most notorious assassin of Julius Caesar. This sweet boy was no Brutus. I renamed him Sonny because he would be my son and my sunshine.

He is NOTHING like Louie. He is not well-behaved, laid-back, or quiet. But so what? He is perfect in a different way. He wants to give away every drop of love he can make, and he's always trying to make more.

The shelter saved a dog that had been adopted and rejected three times, and that unwanted dog has filled my world with life and love.

When it's time to go to sleep, I say, "Cuddle!" Sonny dives under the covers and gets as close to me as he can. He does it every night.

He is now a five-year-old, fifty-three-pound pit bull who has more energy than any dog I have ever seen. He's my best friend, soulmate, and sanity point in a world that has gone batshit crazy. He's wild, energetic, athletic, goofy, erratic, and protective. It took three years to get him to stop pulling on the leash or running away, but now he stays with me off-leash and rarely pulls. Well, sometimes he needs a refresher course on the pulling thing, but he knows what I'm after.

Of all the dogs I have had (and all have been rescues), he's the one most like me. He's a bit of a misfit, but he has the best of intentions. He comes on a little strong, but he means well. He can be a little dorky; I'm a little dorky. He is nosey; I used to be a reporter. He's a rule breaker; I'm a rule breaker. He loves nature, is fearless in his adventures, and is always ready to go. Just like Mommy.

When the Covid-19 lockdown came, I was never lonely living alone. Sonny and my two rescue Ragdoll cats were right with me. We were and are a complete, happy family. I was paired up in relationships most of my adult life but went solo right before Covid and was living single and alone for the first time since I was 26.

What I learned was shocking: Being alone is easy and enjoyable. I prefer it. I LOVE IT. But it works because of my pets.

BRUTUS

Has lived in this cage since 9/26/2019

Brutus here! So listen to *THIS...* I was adopted *and* then given away to someone!! Yup, just given away. I then ended up in another county's shelter!!! <<*gasp*>> Can you believe it?? ☹ Ohhh, but wait, it gets even worse - on top of ALL that - my time was up, I could have died!!!! <<*smh*>> Thank goodness that shelter contacted this shelter, and they let me come back here <<*thankfully*>> Not that I am happy to be in a shelter, but I sure am grateful to be alive; living is way more fun than just Not... I mean, can you imagine no more car rides or take out?? Nope, me neither; so, let's make this official. Just all about me: I am super *sweet, gentle, kind* and *handsome*; I am young, maybe 1.5 years old; and, *I LOVE other dogs!* Naturally, everyone here loves me, and I am so happy that I have a chance to find a new family. I can't wait to be in my own home taking walks, riding in the car, watching TV *and* snuggling with you! ☺ My best life is ahead!!

ID#A091867

**ASK HOW YOU CAN SPEND TIME
WITH BRUTUS**

The card on his shelter cage. "Brutus" is the name of the most notorious assassin of Julius Caesar. He still knows that name.

The card on his shelter cage. "Brutus" is the name of the most notorious assassin of Julius Caesar. He still knows that name.

My cats Coconut and Teddy won't travel—taking them a mile away to the vet is a stressful ordeal that makes *me* want the tranquilizer, so there is no way to bring them across the country. That's why I thought I'd never be able to leave for more than a week.

Enter Jane Nottenburg, a feline-loving friend whose cat had recently passed away. We were at dinner with our friend Nancy, and I was trying to get her to cat-sit for my babies. Nancy said she would do it, "But you won't be getting Coconut back." She meant it!

Jane chimed in, "I will watch your cats *and* I will give them back!"

My life filled with possibility in that moment. I couldn't fall asleep that night because I finally had my solution. I could finally go.

Somewhere. I was going to go somewhere.

I wouldn't be able to do the trip without Sonny. He is my protector and my life partner. He is.

I live in Dunedin, Florida, a scenic town on the West Coast of Florida, north of Clearwater and west of Tampa. Because I share our exploits frequently on Facebook, *everybody* in town knows and loves Sonny. They've seen him kayaking, hiking, running on beaches, camping, swimming, golf carting, attending festivals, getting ice cream, and so much more. He's a character, and everybody knows it, so people on the street regularly honk and shout his name. I have no idea who they are, but they all know Sonny.

Sonny (a.k.a Little Man and on certain days, Ding-Dong) is a lot of things, but he is not a tent camper. I have loved tent camping so much over the years, but he became so exhausted and stressed out trying to protect his mommy from raccoons, armadillos, and other "threats" that I always had to bring him home. Two nights was the limit. He was miserable in a tent.

I had to get an RV. Because of my dog. Not for me, but for him. It's his van. When he sleeps better, I sleep better. As long as he's happy, we can keep going and going.

I CAN'T WAIT

On my fiftieth birthday, I gave myself a mantra: *I will dive fearlessly into this and every moment of my life.* I came up with it as I flew 10,000 feet above Central Florida in a rickety old airplane, preparing to skydive for the first time. I was immediately tested on my mantra when I smelled the breath of the instructor who was my tandem partner. The guy smelled like he'd consumed a fifth of Jack Daniels. *I will dive fearlessly into this and every moment of my life*, I told myself.

We leaped into the air. I did not die. But I did post a bad review on Google.

Since then, I've used that mantra to do so much, like traveling alone in the Middle East or speaking in front of 200,000 people (yeah, that happened).

But before I left on my trip, that mantra had started to feel distant.

I had become a fearful person, and I knew exactly when it happened.

On May 25, 2021, I was cycling three miles from home. A man was walking on the bike path with AirPods in his ears and did a sudden U-turn when he reached his halfway point. I saw him and shouted, but he couldn't hear me, didn't look up, and walked right into my bike, sending me through the air. I remember my head slamming into the pavement, then the police arriving, then the fire truck, and then the ambulance.

Thank God I was wearing a helmet. I most certainly would have died or spent the rest of my life in a vegetative state if I hadn't worn one. Even with the helmet, I suffered a significant head injury.

I have been a serious cyclist since my 20s and by the time of "The Accident," I had cycled about 80,000 miles.

The concussion impacted my memory and processing so severely that I couldn't work for months and struggled for more than a year after that. I forgot so many details of life that I should have easily recalled, and it felt like I was getting worse. I would see people I have known for years and didn't know their names. I couldn't even remember the name of the street I had lived on for nine years and drove on regularly. Michelle Brigman and I were launching our *Hard Won Wisdom* podcast, but I couldn't do the work. Everything stopped.

My neurologist coolly told me it was likely I had early-onset Alzheimer's disease or dementia, prescribed Aricept, the Alzheimer's medication, and ordered a million tests. That was one of the worst moments of my life, particularly since I was at my mother's side for her 12 years of suffering with Alzheimer's.

In the months after my diagnosis, tests finally showed that what was happening in my brain was not Alzheimer's but lingering concussion damage. That neuro instructed me to remain on the Alzheimer's medicine. My primary care doctor, Dr. Julia Jenkins, protects me like a mama bear protects her cubs. Since the lumbar puncture showed no Alzheimer's protein clumps, she strongly encouraged me not to take the medication. So I stopped. The neurologist's PA later told me she agreed with what Dr. J said, but since I couldn't find another neurologist with a good reputation who was taking new patients, I worried I was doing the wrong thing by not taking the medicine.

That is the big reason I wanted to travel NOW, not later.

In the back of my mind, I feared I was on the same track as my mom.

I thought about getting a van and hitting the road. As I kept talking myself in and out of the idea, something big happened.

Wendy Barmore died.

Wendy was Dunedin's resident ass-kicking musician and singer who belted out blues and rock every weekend, everywhere. At 67, she had the youngest spirit and highest cool factor of any of us. She was beloved.

After a performance, Wendy suffered a stroke. There were many surgeries, and one surgery was botched. That caused another stroke, which paralyzed her. And then, she died. That was merciful because she was too much of a force to live in paralysis. But the loss to her family, friends, and community was enormous.

We all remain shocked by it. How was it even possible? Wendy?

Within days, I lost another friend. He was 63. And another. She was 58. And another, 59.

I wondered, how can people in my age group be dying? Heart attacks, cancer, ALS, stroke. How? None of these people expected to die young, but one minute, they were as alive as me and the next, they were dead. I have seven friends in cancer treatment. Wait. Make that eight.

The plan was always to do a big RV trip at age 65, but these recent deaths and my worries about my brain made me question whether I could wait.

My fantasies of travel coincided with my struggle to figure out what to do next with my career. After Wendy died, I needed to stop trying to force the universe to give me answers. I needed to just go live my life.

At first, I focused on going on safari in Africa. But that would last only two or three weeks, and I wanted to disengage for a good bit longer. For years, I've been addicted to YouTube videos on RVers who head out for long stretches, and I had to ask myself, *How long will I have my health? How long will I be able to function on my own?*

My memory was so much better than it had been in the immediate months after my cycling accident, but I still had lapses and worried that I might have been wrong when I chose to stop taking the Alzheimer's medicine.

Every time I'd forget a name, a detail, or a movie title, I'd think, "Here we go…" I wondered if I was losing it.

If I waited—even just a few years—I might not be able to attempt a big road trip. I could get lost thousands of miles from home.

That could happen, right? There was that voice again.

VANNER

June and Bob Gabriel were packed and ready to go again. Every year, they leave for three months, four months, or five months. It just depends. I'm always wistful watching them load up and leave, and they know I'm longing to do it, too.

"Why don't you let go of that big house and just go?" June asked. "It ties you down. Just think of the freedom you could have…"

Freedom. She said that word in a way no one else does. She knows something the rest of us don't. She and Bob have been retired for years and aren't controlled by things but are liberated by moments. Nothing is as valuable as freedom.

I've been a self-employed writer and speaker for 25 years, and I have a lot of freedom. If I choose to kayak during the day, I can write late into the night. No big deal.

Listening to June always made me wistful. She and Bob have not lived according to plan. They've just lived. The freedom June was talking about meant embracing boundless possibility in a spontaneous, untethered life.

That scared the hell out of me.

June and Bob are my RV gurus. Over the years, they've had three pop-ups, one truck camper, a fifth wheel, a Class C Mercedes, two trailers, and "too many tents to remember." Long ago, June started urging me to think bigger and head out into the wilds.

"Just think of the freedom," she'd say.

She kept saying that word "freedom," but I'd always tell myself, "I can't do that yet."

June would say, "Why not?"

When I started thinking more about that freedom thing, I was perplexed by how I'd pull it off.

"I can't figure out what to do," I said one night. "What kind of RV is right for me?"

June didn't hesitate.

"You need a van," she said. "That will give you the ultimate freedom."

Vans are different from trailers and motorhomes because they are so much easier to drive and maneuver. The mileage is substantially better, and you can stop and camp stealth in a multitude of places.

Plus, vans are cool.

Want a good deal on a used camping van? Good luck. I scoured online, but everything was too expensive, had too many miles, or looked crappy.

Buying a new one was preposterous. I don't do debt, and it seemed like the new ones all cost more than $125,000. I didn't want to clear out that much cash.

Deciding what to do was frustrating, and Patri, my neighbor, shared that frustration. Patri and I walk our lookalike, best-friend dogs every day. She also wanted to traipse across the country with her dog. All we talked about was vans, vans, vans. We went to the Florida RV SuperShow in Tampa (the largest RV show in the world) and exhausted ourselves checking out vans we could never afford.

We test-drove vans at Lazydays RV center. Patri tried the Winnebago Solis Pocket 36A, which I considered way too small. But she made me test drive it, and I fell in love with it. It *was* too small. But it was also so easy to drive, got good mileage, and could fit in any parking space.

I started looking for used ones.

This dragged on, and one day I found a smoking good deal on new Winnebago Solis Pocket 36A vans at a dealership outside of San Antonio, Texas. Patri and I negotiated together to get a great price for two vans. We planned to fly to Texas, and then drive them back to Florida.

I wondered if I could get a dealer in Florida to match that price, and guess what? It worked.

Patri and I bought twin vans on the same day from the same dealer in the same deal. We squealed and danced like nerdy schoolgirls when we picked them up in Port Saint Lucie, Florida. We took dozens of videos and pictures, and I think I was giddier than I have ever been about anything in my life. I was so distracted and excited that I didn't pay attention when we were shown how everything worked. I'm usually so focused when signing paperwork, but I wasn't focused at all. That poor woman in the contract department—I am sure my joy was annoying as hell.

Why weren't the people at the dealership as excited as we were? I guess it was just another day at work for them, but we were leaping into the next chapters of our lives.

Patri's brother warned her not to drive home with the wrong van and the wrong dog because, if not for Sonny's wild streak, it could happen! Our vans are basic: no bathrooms, no generators. Small, but still just right. Solar batteries can power everything but the air conditioner. They have fridges, two-burner stoves, and sinks.

They were new and would do the job. Most important, the price was right.

Every day, thousands of people buy fancy RVs on credit and are instantly underwater with the debt. They lose 25 percent of the value driving off the lot, and since RV owners are notorious for never finding the perfect RV, they keep trading their rigs in and making their debt problems worse. People take out 20-year loans for RVs and get sucked in with low interest rates, not thinking that they are attaching themselves to a $150,000 or $200,000 debt for a depreciating asset. Also, there is a lot of garbage out there that looks nice on the lot or at the RV show but falls apart quickly. It's unlikely a van is going to live to be a healthy 20 years old, and when it dies, those who took out those long-term RV mortgages are going to be making payments on something that is dead, dead, dead.

We bought our vans for $69,000 each. Once all the taxes and tags were added in, they cost $74,652. That's a great price on a van—and a big ouch for me. But we spent what we were willing to spend, bought the vans with cash, and made peace with the limits of what we bought. We left owing nothing to a bank.

We could drive anywhere, stop, cook dinner, get a good night's sleep, then move right along to the next place. We camped near the dealership at the Savannas Preserve State Park that first night, so exhausted but still ridiculously giddy. I love Patri, but I didn't want to make conversation with her. I wanted to sit in my van. I couldn't believe it! It was all mine.

I couldn't sleep in my van that night. I was too amped up.

I wanted to get going.

WHERE?

An hour after I brought my van home, I sat on my living room couch, pulled out the Rand McNally Road Atlas, and opened it to the US map.

"Okay. Where?" I said aloud.

I could go anywhere on that map. Anywhere.

I was free.

I wasn't just dreaming up a big camping trip. I was chucking my career—for the moment and perhaps forever in its present form. I was saying, "That's it. I'm going to do what I've been terrified of doing. I'm going to let go."

Where? Where to?

It was so obvious. I would head to Colorado, where I'd spent most of my 30s and where I still have a posse of friends. I've cycled almost every mountain pass there, which makes me feel intimately connected to the Rockies. I moved back to Florida 26 years ago for my family and the warm weather, but Colorado has always been my other home.

Okay, where else?

Wyoming. I've got to do Wyoming. Then Montana. I've got to cycle there. Then into Canada to Banff, Lake Louise, and Jasper. I'd shoot across middle America until I got to North Carolina for a couple of weeks in the Great Smoky Mountains before heading home. I had no specifics. I knew I'd go to Arlington, Texas, on the way out to see Michelle, my podcast partner, and I'd see other Texas friends. Then I'd head to Colorado.

Would I go through Amarillo? I have an old friend there. And maybe take a detour to Albuquerque? Friends and an ex are there. Or head to Colorado from Texas? Once in Colorado, would I go to Denver first or to Southwest Colorado, where the best mountains are? I had no plan. Just to get to Colorado and hike, cycle, and be.

I was not raised to be spontaneous, outdoorsy, or athletic, but I am. My parents never camped. They lived according to plan and did not fish, dive, kayak, hike, camp, or boat. They were the best people I have ever known, but in their minds, a vacation was about going back to Michigan to see relatives or going to the beach for a few days. We did a few big trips when I was a kid. Yellowstone once, Florida a few times, and of course, the Smokies. But Mom never went beyond the US or Canada. Dad was from Germany and served in the military overseas, but he didn't crave big travel, either. They were set in their lives. These were not people who would get vanlife.

But they did get me. They encouraged my travels as long as I stayed in touch so they knew I was safe.

I have seen a lot of the world. My career as a speaker has taken me all over North America, South America, Europe, the Middle East, and Asia. My adventures have taken me all over the place, too. When I was married, my husband and I made an annual trip to Europe. When we divorced, I couldn't afford it anymore and started weeklong bike trips with friends where we'd cycle a different state, camping along the way. I discovered that the joy of travel had little to do with where I was. It was about *who* I became in those hours that weren't colored by my job. And it was about who I was with.

I looked at that atlas, and my world opened.

Everything was about to change. I could feel it.

PANIC PACKING

The inside of my suitcase has always looked like the back of the Clampetts' truck. Overstuffed, chaotic, and so disorganized I cannot find anything. I have spent more than two decades traveling for work, and it never gets any better.

I had to pack my van for three months of travel. I was no better at packing that small van than I was at packing my carry-on. It was a disaster.

Patri, a retired doctor, maintains a house in California, so she left town a month before I did when the Florida snowbird season ended. We planned to hang out with each other in Montana and then go to Canada for a couple of days before splitting off. Watching her panic pack made me stress out, too. We were buying bins, drawers, and containers to create storage, but something seemed off.

All of those storage solutions ate up storage. I don't want to speak for Patri, but I was in denial about what I couldn't live without, and the more I stuffed into my van, the more I thought I was outsmarting my space limitations.

My Amazon cart consistently had another $200 or $300 worth of stuff. That was for multiple orders every week. Every time I hit the buy button, I felt anxiety because I knew I was probably wasting my money. It was so constant that I would tense up every time I saw a delivery person arrive with a big box (or four). I almost always had no idea what I'd even ordered.

Here is some of the madness. Flip flops, car phone mount, travel bed for Sonny, collapsible dish drying rack, Samsung Galaxy tablet, sheets, headphones, knee brace, phone case, egg holder, multi-spice shaker, collapsible food storage containers, laundry sheets, three-quart Instant Pot, gel cushion, car wash brush kit, poop bags (1,000 of them), unbreakable hand mirror, rechargeable LED flashlights, paper towel holder, rechargeable fan, AirTags, steering wheel lock, small combination safe, hiking boots, cargo carrier with bike rack, travel dog bowl, bike chain lock, RV water pressure regulator, Swedish dishcloths, memory foam mattress, portable air compressor, wheel chocks, heavy duty extension cables, portable power station, bike tubes, bike tires, lip gloss, RV fuses, seat cushion, dog food, camping towels… There were so many more items, but that is just a little of the insanity.

Patri and I faced the same challenge: cramming everything into a seventeen-foot Ram Promaster van. I needed hoses, electrical equipment, batteries, clothes, bedding, winter coats, umbrellas, bike clothes, shoes, and more shoes for every possible sport. I packed first aid and medical supplies—waaay too much. But how would I know what I wouldn't need? I also needed my bike, helmet, tire pump, kayak, paddle, and life jacket, hiking poles, hiking boots, umbrella, a bunch of books and…

Ugh. "I need, I need, I need…"

I kept thinking of something else I had to fit in the van. I probably should have thrown in a pair of jeans, two pairs of shorts, some T-shirts, every pair of underwear I owned, and headed out. But I was microplanning for every contingency. I brought the Instant Pot because I didn't know how someone like me (who barely cooks) could live without one for three months. I brought my smoothie maker because I love smoothies. I wanted to have a television so I could watch downloaded Netflix movies, but I was conflicted about that because the whole point was to disengage from my devices. So I bought a Samsung Galaxy tablet that would let me stream everything I wanted and installed a mount next to my bed.

Would I get bored by myself? I had a lot of friends to see along the way, but I'd also have more solitude than I had ever experienced. Better bring a bunch of books.

I looked forward to being alone. I'm an introvert. I recharge alone. I don't sleep well with anyone in my space who is not a significant other (when I have one) or my dog. I love when it's just me and Sonny, and I don't sleep well without him.

I never feel lonely and figured I would write or read, play with Sonny, nap, go for walks, whatever. There would always something fun to be done. I invited friends to join me for parts of the trip, but they'd have to stay in hotels, not with me in the van. Sonny and I would stay in the parking lot.

The other end of the spectrum was Patri, who would have friends traveling with her and sleeping in her van for much of her trip. What on earth was she thinking? I had the same van, and it was a tight squeeze for me and Sonny. If I had a travel partner, we would have needed straightjackets because there was no space for an extra person. Some people cram in visitors, having them bunk on the dinky couch (feet have to hang over the end) or on a crazy blow-up bed that fits over the front seats. Not. In. My. Van.

Patri's was going to be like a youth hostel with all those people coming and going. I started calling it the clown van.

Seeing her frantic last dash stressed *me* out. Granted, her situation was tighter than mine because her brother was going to be with her for two weeks, so she had his ginormous suitcase and backpack in there. It all must have fit because she drove off and he was still with her.

I waved as they drove away, but I was not envious.

I was grateful that I had four more weeks to figure out how I would load my van, which bugged the hell out of me every single day.

MY SUPERPOWER

The weekend after Patri left, I confronted one of my weaknesses.

Because my van has no bathroom, I had to make peace with doing something that every woman avoids.

The one thing we do not want to do in public—ever—is poop. It is the least ladylike thing there is. When we get a new job, the first thing we do is look for the secret bathroom where we can poop privately and no one's going to recognize our shoes.

When I bought my van that had only a little porta-potty, I knew I was going to have to poop in public.

I was camping with friends on a weekend trip when I announced my new mantra: "Pooping is my superpower."

We have to poop every day, and so I vowed I was going to make peace with it.

My friends took a nap, and I thought, "I'm going to go and poop now. Pooping is my superpower."

I went into the campground bathroom, and there were three stalls. Stall No. 1 and stall No. 3 were occupied, which left the middle one for me. Between two people. For pooping.

I reminded myself there was no need to worry. Doing this in public restrooms was going to be necessary while I traveled. It is just a bodily function. Everybody does it. Instead of cringing at this, I chose it as my superpower. That was that. What difference did it make? The people I'd encounter would all be strangers (who also poop), I reminded myself.

It was a "flush as you go" experience for me, out of courtesy for the others.

The woman in stall No. 1 flushed and left.

When the other one flushed, I thought, "Oh, thank God. I'm in the clear." But she dawdled at the sink, brushing her teeth and doing God knows what, and I was sitting there on the toilet, waiting for her to vacate the premises so I could leave.

She didn't go. If I didn't have the guts to leave while she was still in there, I might be stuck on that toilet for an hour. So I flushed and reminded myself, "Pooping is my superpower."

I left the stall.

She was at the sink, but I was confident in my superpower and didn't care. Not until she turned, cocked her head, and looked me in the eyes. Then she said the worst thing she could ever have said.

"*Fawn?*" she asked.

Noooooooooooooooooo!

It was Traci from my kayaking club.

In that moment, I realized pooping was not my superpower.

GOING IT ALONE

What I should not have done alone:

Well, lots of things.

It's a miracle I wasn't killed years ago while cross-country skiing on top of Rabbit Ears Pass in Colorado. It was late in the day, and the snow was fresh and deep. I was so inexperienced that I thought I was taking a shortcut and wound up in snow that swallowed me to my chest. I somehow had the wherewithal to "swim" up to the surface of the snow, find my skis, and slide down the side of the mountain without starting an avalanche—which was a real possibility.

And there was the time I was cross-country skiing in a seldom-skied backcountry wilderness area and my knee popped. When I tried to stand, I fainted. I lay in the snow, wishing I had cell service up there and wondering who I would call. After almost two hours, two women skiers emerged from the trees and saw me on the ground. They walked me out of there with one arm draped over each woman's shoulder.

I once started a long hike at 3 p.m. on an unseasonably warm fall day in Colorado. I'd planned for a three-mile hike with my dog, but it was so beautiful, I turned it into a 10-mile hike. This was before smart-phones with weather apps, and I found myself at the bottom of the canyon, hours from my car, when the weather turned. The temperature plummeted, and it began snowing. I was in shorts and a T-shirt. Buster, a sheepdog mix, stopped his usual wandering and led me up the wet and slippery trail. We arrived shortly after dark. After he died, I flew his ashes back to Colorado and spread them on that trail.

There are so many stories of me going it alone and doing fine. I camped, hiked, kayaked, alone for most of my life. But in my late 40s and early 50s, I stopped doing it. I went through a cautious phase, choosing to always have someone with me when I adventured. Pairing up was entertaining and responsible. It also kept me from doing what I wanted to do when I wanted to do it.

"If you want to see Fawn happy, just roll her in the dirt," one friend said of me. True.

Unfortunately, few of my friends and none of my partners saw the charm in tent camping. When I was in my "bring a buddy" phase, I did not camp.

But I craved it. I love the first sounds of morning and the first sounds of night. I love seeing trees and nature when I open my eyes. The fragrance of a forest—particularly in the morning—is heavenly.

I would plead, but no one would go with me.

About a decade ago, I realized it was on me to go it alone. I got a campsite next to the Gulf of Mexico, and I felt high driving down there with my dog Louie in the back seat. I was so excited! I set up my tent, inflated my double-decker queen-sized Coleman air mattress, and was in business.

Ten minutes later, a massive thunderstorm blew in—one of those biblical Florida storms that make it impossible to see or move outdoors, and scary because the thunder and lightning cracked all around us and we were in the woods. Louie and I stretched out on the bed, and it wasn't long before water seeped in through the bottom of the tent.

It was fabulous!

If I was comfortable in those conditions, I knew I was good for the duration. The rain stopped, and the skies cleared in time for a wild sunset to burst through the clouds.

After that, I camped all the time. I realized how much fun I had missed waiting for other people to join me. I tent-camped at least a dozen times every year. The more I did it, the easier it became. I was confident that if anything went wrong, I'd figure it out.

Tent camping with Sonny

I missed out on other opportunities in life because I didn't want to go it alone. Time has taught me that was a mistake.

I stayed in some relationships way too long, and because I'd been paired up most of my adult life, it felt more comfortable than what I feared it would be like solo. But at 58, my last break-up happened, and I embraced my aloneness. I found out something that shocked me: I loved being alone. *Loved it.* I loved that I could decide everything I wanted to do, when I wanted to eat, what I wanted to eat, where I wanted to go, what time I wanted to hit the sack, what I wanted to watch on TV, who I wanted to hang out with—I loved pretty much everything about being alone and still love it.

A friend is worried about being alone because her husband is older than she is and is getting up there. I tell her that being alone is a chance for her to discover who she is when she's not having to be there for everybody else.

"When you want a baked potato for dinner, you eat a baked potato," I said.

"What about cereal?" she asked.

"Oh yes. There are cereal nights, too!"

I found real power when I realized I am capable of doing anything I want to do, whether I'm with somebody—or not.

What was it that held me back? Why had I been afraid to be alone, whether it involved pitching a tent or leaving a relationship that needed to end? I underestimated my power. I didn't realize that I was a self-contained unit, capable of taking care of myself.

There is safety in numbers, but there is *power* in the confidence that comes with daring to go it alone. And the best way for me to build that confidence is exposure therapy—doing what scares me over and over until it's no longer scary. I don't like uncertainty, but I don't run from it because, looking back on my life, the greatest magic manifested when I held my breath and took the risk. Even some of those foolhardy risks from my Colorado days taught me big lessons. Everything worked out.

At this point, I have no intention of waiting for someone else to join me because I realize we are all running out of time. If I want to do something, I need to do it now.

I am not all-powerful. I know I will make mistakes. But I'm good being solo for now. Some of my friends feel sorry for me, but I feel sorry for anyone who hasn't experienced this. It can be challenging, but the reward is huge. Self-sufficiency breeds self-confidence. And that makes me strong.

THE GUN THING

Should I bring a gun? Everybody asks, and I agonized about whether to get one.

My mind did a number on me, creating and focusing on unrealistic doubts and fears that made it seem like a gun was a necessity. What if, what if, what if? I kept imagining every town's psycho killer knowing where I was and coming to kill me. Or a bunch of rednecks messing with me because they wanted to scare me.

I bought bear spray (which will stop a bear or psychopath 20 to 30 feet away) and a stun gun. I have my protective black-and-white pit bull, who would be enough of a deterrent for most weirdos. I bought a new iPhone with satellite GPS in case I need to make an emergency call. I had a full-sized spare tire mounted under the van (the van only provided a tire inflation kit!) in case of a flat. I upgraded my AAA membership for 200-miles of RV towing. I set my phone to share my location with my big brother and about 10 other friends. What else did I need to do?

Well, the obvious.

Get a gun.

I do not judge people who have guns for protection. It's something that I have always chosen not to do, but faced with spending nights in the wide open and a mind that was ruminating endlessly on the what-ifs, I started to think it was time.

This trip was not as simple as going to nice Florida state park campgrounds filled with docile retirees. I was going to be camping alone many times, and I was always going to be driving into the unknown.

So, I took gun training. One of the women in my outdoors club set up a training day, and the timing was perfect. I recorded a video of it, and it shows me wincing at the sound of guns firing in the background. I've fired guns, and I'm a good shot, but I never considered getting one until I started planning my travels.

. . .

The training made me feel confident about gun handling, safety, and use. But I still couldn't make up my mind, so I posted this on Facebook:

I strongly believe in gun control. But the idea of spending extended time in the wilds in my van this summer has made me question if I need a firearm. My kayaking/adventure club had a ladies' day gun training yesterday, and I went out to shoot. It was interesting to see how the others reacted. I can't make up my mind about this. In my brain, I know that one more person with a weapon makes the problem worse. In my heart, I feel that a woman traveling by herself (even with a protective dog) needs more than a stun gun or a taser. I would love to know your thoughts. I'm not going to say what I ultimately decide because that feels private. But the conversation would be helpful.

Here are some of the nearly 90 responses I received:

. . .

Val: My Dad always told me if you own a gun, you have to be prepared for the time you must use it. "Are you prepared to come face to face with someone and kill them?" he asked. I was not. "Are you prepared to have an intruder take it from you and kill you because you were hesitant to kill him first?" he asked. I was speechless.

Mike: Are you willing to spend the rest of your life remembering the head of the guy you shot exploding when you fired your gun to protect yourself?

Amy: I suggest bear spray (learn how to properly use it), which I backpack with and keep in the vehicle/camper. I also carry a belt loop pepper spray when hiking or going to events. The idea is to incapacitate the creep until you can get away. If that's not enough, check out stun guns, but they have their own challenges. You will do far better by observing your surroundings, taking safety precautions (locks, lights, location, etc.), and introducing yourself to your camping neighbors. Also, attitude is paramount, meaning, don't present yourself as a scared, meek victim. Look the perp straight in the eye and observe what he looks like and what he's wearing. Safety courses say that if you act demure and avoid eye contact, it emboldens the perp. Women tend to look away, shrink, look frightened, slink away, etc.—exactly what the guy is looking for. Keep your cell phone handy for photos, 911, etc. Lastly, take a self-defense course.

Carol: I am a strong advocate for gun control. I was nearly 50 when I bought my first firearm. I now own a handgun, a hunting rifle, and a shotgun. I have a farm, and I feel like I'm adequately covered for home and livestock defense, humane animal dispatch, and hunting, which I rarely do. I am about as left as one can lean, and here I am with a veritable arsenal. It is a controversial and private subject and very personal.

· · ·

Wendy: Criminals aren't out prowling through the woods looking for victims. You'd be more likely to be the victim of a crime of opportunity and in most cases that crime will involve wanting your property more than to harm you (serial killers aren't hanging out on forest land). So consider whether you're willing to kill someone over your insured van. And what the chances are that the rare person who might commit a crime of opportunity in the wild is likely to approach a camper with a pit bull present.

Barbara: I lived alone on the road—with my dog—in my 30-foot Class A motorcoach for more than six years, and in that time, I had numerous fairly intense adventures. Never had to actually shoot my Smith and Wesson .38 pistol. There was one event when I'd pulled over to the side of the highway so my dog could pee, and a group of very rough-looking men pulled up beside me. Their expressions were definitely NOT offering help or support! Just in case, just before they reached me, I pulled that little pistol out of my pocket and watched them all panic and flee! You can tell by body language and facial expressions when someone's up to no good. I absolutely advise you to carry a gun when you are alone and clearly vulnerable!

Arnold: You have a gun and make a mistake, someone gets killed. If you don't...

Other than that, if you're considering going places where you'll need a gun to feel safe, consider going elsewhere. If someone forces you to make the shoot/don't shoot decision, while you're deciding, he's firing. She who hesitates is shot. Don't put yourself in that position if you're not made for it.

One private message from my friend Laci helped me a lot because it came from a fellow van camper who has been on the road for more than a year. "I also believe in gun control and grew up with guns. We chose to not travel with one in the van and use strategically placed canisters of bear spray. They're much easier to use and you don't have to have precision and consistent training that a gun requires. Also, I don't want to have to carry the trauma of killing a human even if they're trying to do harm to me. I would much rather blind them with bear spray to achieve the goal of getting away."

All of that feedback helped me. It was such a big issue because the wrong decision could result in someone else's death. Or mine. If I don't carry a gun in Florida—where guns are so plentiful and nearly three million people have concealed weapons permits—why would I carry one where I would encounter few other people?

I wasn't sure I would or could shoot to kill. I imagined I'd hesitate, which would defeat the purpose.

None of it felt right for me.

THERE IS NO PLAN

You've seen the photo on the internet: A stereotypical white van surrounded by red sandstone formations that rise against a desert landscape…

I've seen that dreamy picture so many times. I've certainly imagined myself in that white van.

That is, until I jolted awake at 3 a.m., drowning in anxiety, realizing I had no idea where I would be camping. I'd thought I was going to be a true vanlifer and try the 250 million acres of public land where we can camp for free. But my anxiety made it clear that was not how I would be camping.

I did not want to camp alone on 250 million acres where nobody would know where I was. I don't mind hiking alone—I've always done that. But the idea of falling asleep where there would be no other person for miles rattled me. It made me feel vulnerable and exposed, certain that if there were one psycho within 100 miles, he'd head straight to my van to kill me and Sonny.

I want campgrounds or parking lots around people. Campgrounds are great because if I need help, I can get it. Also, many campgrounds come with amenities known to civilization as showers and flush toilets. I always say you should do what scares you until it no longer scares you, but this was not something I wanted to become comfortable with.

This was my 3 a.m. reckoning. I needed more of a plan and had waited so long that it would be impossible to arrange camping reservations in the busy summer season.

At 3:30 a.m., I posted my concerns on a vanlife forum. By the end of the day, I had about 50 messages from people telling me not to worry and just expect everything to work out. Three of the posters said I was a wimp. One person said I would never have the "true" vanlife experience if I didn't use public lands.

Uh, wait a minute.

Who is to define what my "true" vanlife experience is?

That silliness reminds me of my screenwriting teacher who criticized a friend's science fiction writing. "As an aficionado of time travel," the teacher said, "I can tell you that you have violated all of the rules."

The rules of time travel. Ron had violated the rules of time travel.

As absurd as the rules of true vanlife.

I am disengaging so I can make my own rules. My first rule would be, "I will gladly violate the rules of true vanlife."

A lot of vanlifers have a cliché recipe for show. It's where they go, how they film themselves, what they post, and how they project their cool factor. They have a picture of the van in front of an incredible backdrop. They post a picture taken from inside the van with the back doors opening to a breathtaking view. And there is always the shot of them sitting on the van roof watching the sunset.

Am I "less than" because I want to camp around people? Was I doing this to be like *them* or to be like *me*?

This was an important conversation in my head because I was not doing this trip for show. I was doing it to find the me that I'd lost. There would be no way to do that by trying to be like everybody else.

I was a woman who had started to feel old. I wanted to be in the mountains, away from the Florida heat, and surrounded by fresh air and quiet nature. I wanted to be athletic. I wanted to talk to old friends and figure out what all of our years apart had added up to. I wanted to know who I was going to be for the rest of my life.

I had to trust that I'd figure out the camping details as I went along. That was unsettling, but I remembered traipsing through Europe with a backpack and a Eurail pass when I was in my 20s. I never knew where I was going to go or where I was going to stay. I never had a reservation.

That was one of the most magical times in my life.

I was free, my very best self, and it always worked out.

I will be free, my very best self.

And it will all work out.

ALL CLEAR

I often dictate my journal, and this one entry blows my mind. I was walking Sonny a week before my departure, and I felt sentimental about leaving home.

"I'm tempted to say 'Screw it' and not go," I said. "I know this experience will push me to my limits and help me to define the rest of my life. That's all new and exciting. But I like what I have here. I love home. Five minutes from kayaking in the Gulf of Mexico. A mile's walk to the Intracoastal, where I can watch the sunset every night if I want. I am longing to stay here, and I don't think that is fear talking."

Then I wrestled with it. "No. I can't know what is out there unless I go out there. I can't grow doing what I always do. I'm 62 and, by the time I get back, I will be on the brink of 63. I will blink my eyes, and then I will be 73 and then 83. How am I going to fill those years? By doing what I always do? NO. If I'm going to do anything big and exhausting, the time to do it is now.

"And if I get out there and find that I'd rather be home in Dunedin, well, that is valuable information, too."

The two weeks before leaving were filled with kayaking, sunrises and sunsets, time with friends, and time enjoying beautiful Dunedin. I really was sad leaving home.

I had one big piece of last-minute business: an appointment with a neurologist.

My memory was still a big question mark. I wanted a better neurologist, but the two five-star neuros in this area weren't taking new patients. Then someone told me about a great neurologist who was new to the same practice as the five-star guys. Seeing Dr. Leana Oppenheim was the last big thing on my checklist. I wanted to go before I left so she could order the in-depth Alzheimer's tests that are scheduled months in advance. I'd do the testing after I returned.

She listened intently to my story about my accident and my memory loss. She reviewed my scary CT scan and the MRI, which was better. Then she gave me the Mini-Mental State Examination, which is the screening tool for Alzheimer's and dementia. The other neurologist, who told me I likely had early onset Alzheimer's or dementia, hadn't even given me that most basic test.

Afterward, she leaned forward in her chair and said, "You have a perfect score. You do not have Alzheimer's. You do not have dementia. You should never have been put on that medicine. You don't need more testing. You don't need to come back—unless something changes."

I can still hear her saying that.

I was shocked. And so relieved and grateful. I'd spent so long fearing I had a memory disorder and was convinced it wouldn't be long before I started getting lost. I feared I soon wouldn't be able to travel.

It turns out my memory lapses are good ol' senior moments! The long-lasting brain fog I experienced after the accident was a serious concussion.

I will love that doctor forever. The world *was* open to me. Wander Woman Fawn Germer was on her way into the unknown.

That night, I met my friends Jean and Sarah at the marina, and it was a nice sunset with champagne. When Sarah was leaving, she hugged me and said, "I mean this. If there is trouble, no matter where you are, I can come to you. There is nowhere you will be that I cannot get to and help you if you need me to. Just call me." She's a Brit and is director of global security for a behemoth international corporation. She knows people who get things done all over the world, so I felt like I had the power of an army behind me, and that was Sarah. SHE would come for me.

She made me feel safe.

LAST-MINUTE CHAOS

"Sixty-one, sixty-eight," Oprah said, pointing at Tina Turner, then Cher. "I mean, it's just really unbelievable. How do you feel about getting older?"

"I think it sucks!" the inimitable Cher blurted.

Turner burst out laughing.

"What about all the wisdom..." Oprah said.

"Oh f**k that!" said Cher with a laugh.

Mmmm-hmmm. There are moments when it really does suck.

I'd come back from the Y after swimming a little over a mile, sat at my desk, and then stood up to get something to drink.

BAM!

My left knee hyperextended, and I slammed to the ground as my artificial knee replacement buckled backward. I was able to get up, but I knew something was very wrong.

My brain went wild. That fall could have happened while I was hiking. *I could have hit my head on a rock. I could have been stranded out there, alone, with no way out...*

I couldn't get into my orthopedic surgeon's office for a week. The knee was swollen, making it obvious that my plans for hiking and long-distance cycling in the Rockies were likely doomed.

"This could change everything," I wrote in my journal. "I need to calm down, figure it out, and adapt. What am I going to do? The one thing I am definitely not going to do is stay home. I am going."

I brainstormed.

"I will drink in the scenery and enjoy my friends. I'll kayak. I'll have time to think and read and write. Maybe I'll start writing another novel. I can work. Write letters to people I love. I can use the time to go deep spiritually. Go to yoga classes like I've never wanted to do. And hit the Ys and swim. It'll all work out."

My motto in a crisis: Accept, cope, adapt. I started the process immediately.

When I finally went to the orthopedic surgeon, he said my knee replacement needed surgical revision. It may need a full replacement—they wouldn't know until they looked inside. UGH!

"No can do," I said. "I'm going to be traveling in my van in the mountains all summer. I leave Friday. It's nonnegotiable."

"Here are the rules," he said. "You have to *always* wear a brace when you are walking or hiking. Only hike the easiest trails—the paved ones. Ice it and take ibuprofen for swelling. When you feel pain, *stop*."

That was a long list of rules to give to a rule breaker, but he didn't tell me to stay home.

The next day, I received a speeding ticket. I'd just switched insurance companies, so that ticket meant one big thing about my trip: No speeding, not ever.

The unfairness of this is annoying. I'm always a slowpoke driver. I drive so slow that people won't let me take them to the airport. That cop got me on one of the few times when I was rushing like crazy to get things done because I was leaving town for three months. And true —I *was* speeding. But I have a friend who gets pulled over at least every other year, and she does all that fake crying and always gets a warning. I rarely speed, and I won't fake cry because I refuse to act like a helpless female, and I get the ticket.

So I was in a really good mood when the next thing happened.

Hoping to get my tires checked before leaving, I hopped into the van—you know, the brand new one with 3,000 miles on it—and the air conditioner wouldn't blow cold. It was June, and I wondered at first whether the van was taking extra long to cool down in the Florida heat. But it wasn't cooling at all. Then, when I pulled onto the street, the power steering wouldn't work. I struggled to control the wheel so I could make it around the block to come back home. Then the battery light came on.

Something was very wrong, and I was leaving in 43 hours! Even though I expected that the problem would be covered under the warranty, I had no faith in Ram getting it fixed quickly. The company had a huge problem with parts in its supply chain. I've spared you those stories, but I'd already gone many rounds on everything from radios to screws. They know me at corporate.

I worried I'd never get out of Dunedin.

"Do not drive that van. You need a tow," said the technician at the dealership when I called.

I had to use the first allowable tow on my new AAA card—one of two tows allowed for the year—and I hadn't even left home.

Bye-bye van.

Well, whatever. I learned a long time ago that when nobody is sick, it's not really a problem. Just an issue. I was annoyed and anxious, and sure, I wouldn't get to leave on Friday and that would delay everything. Again, whatever. It would delay my planned start for a trip that barely had a plan.

I accepted I was in a situation out of my control, then went to the beach to swim at sunset.

It was not just any sunset. This was one of the most fiery, astonishing, awe-filled sunsets I have ever seen. My stress dissolved. I swam at Honeymoon Island State Park, which is 10 minutes from home, took pictures, and felt deep gratitude for that beautiful moment. I was sad to be leaving my paradise.

For a couple of hours, I stopped worrying.

What about the van? How long was the repair going to take? Would I be able to go Friday? Monday? What was wrong?

It was out of my control, so why worry? I'm always telling myself that. What I could control was that I had a perfect evening in one of my favorite places on earth. I was happy and at peace.

"Your van is ready," the shop tech said when he called me at 11 a.m.

Seriously? It was that quick? The breakdown was a big deal problem with a quick fix. My serpentine belt had fallen off. It was not an expensive part, but it was a BIG deal part because that rubber belt sends power to the alternator, power steering pump, air conditioner, and water pump. When that belt fell off, I had a total system shutdown.

All the dealership did was put the *same* serpentine belt back on. This is the belt that failed me and completely disabled my van. They said "It slipped off. Everything is fine."

Now, how much confidence would anyone have in that? I didn't have *any* confidence in it. This Ram Promaster 1500 van was my first American-made vehicle, and for it to lock up like that instantly destroyed my trust in my rolling home. Still, the dealership was not going to give me a new belt, no way. I even talked to my contact in the executive office at Ram's parent company. If I wanted to start my trip in this century, I had to pick up my van and hope for the best.

I prepared to leave in 20 hours, as planned.

The delay cost me a day of packing, so I had an even madder rush to get ready. I was in and out of the van, doing all of my work in terrible heat. I was covered in old lady bruises—the ones that look terrible but you have no idea where they came from.

I was grouchy, nervous, and not ready. But I was leaving in the morning. Time was up.

Before I fell asleep, I wrote this:

"I want to write something profound because tomorrow, my life changes. I leave on my big adventure. But I am so tired—I just want to sleep. So this is what I have to say: I am going to miss home. My home. My town. The sunsets. My kayak. But home is where you are, and I am outahere."

PART 2: ROAD TRIP

WANNA GO FOR A RIDE?

Sonny is so nervous watching out the front window as I load all my clothes and gear this week, and I am certain he's worried that I'm going somewhere and leaving him behind.

"Go for a ride?" I finally ask.

He flies out the front door, into the van, and onto his couch in the back in a single leap. Little Man doesn't know where he is going—all he cares is that he's going there with me.

We drive away like it's no big deal. Like we're heading to Tampa or something. But I am soaring! The minute I leave the driveway, I go from high anxiety to no anxiety.

I have no responsibilities! Is there something I'm supposed to be worrying about? Don't speed. Don't hit anybody. Don't get hit by anybody. Don't run out of gas...

I am so close to home, but I'm already so far gone.

I still don't have much of a plan. I'm going to Pete's house in the Panhandle tonight, then most of the way to Arlington, Texas to see Michelle, Karin, and the gang, then Colorado, Wyoming, Montana, and Canada.

I'm not sure how I will route out of Texas, if I will go to New Mexico, who I will visit, what I will do … I have no idea. I have a handful of campground reservations over the next three months, and I have to get to Tina's house for her 50th anniversary party in three weeks. Doug and Teri will meet me August 2 in Canada, but other than that, nothing is set.

For the first time, I am going to make up my life one minute at a time. If I feel like going, I will go. If I feel like stopping, I will stop. If I want to take a detour, I will take a detour.

I feel hopeful. Free!

Heading out

I feel young. Wow. Already?

Yesssss! I feel so young.

We make it to Santa Rosa Beach to visit Pete Foley, my friend since we were both reporters in Jacksonville in our 20s. I want to see a familiar face on my first night out. It's a reminder that I will know people along the way, that I won't be alone.

I've driven almost 400 miles, past rolling hills, quaint towns, and so many fields of horses and cows. I see his familiar porch, and his front door swings open when I pull into the driveway. There's Pete, arms wide. He hands me a glass of wine, and I see the charcuterie.

It's not just a greeting. It's a welcome home, a perfect Panhandle sunset.

DISCONNECTING

After sleeping hard in Pete's driveway, I'm up early and heading out, singing "What's Going On?" as loud as I can, then Aretha's "Respect" full blast. I belt out "Sweet Home Alabama" because it comes on just as I cruise across the Alabama border—how about that?

I expected to rush through my Deep South driving to get to the good part of my trip, but these long drives *are* the good part of my trip. Who knew that driving in the middle of nowhere thinking about notadamnthing could be so therapeutic?

I arrive at the Beaver Dam Campground in Minden, Louisiana, only four hours from Dallas. I can't drive another mile.

I'm not one to complain (much), but this campground is the most humid, hell-hot place I have *ever* been. No breathing allowed in Louisiana, and the mosquitos?!?! They are giant, hungry, blood-sucking beasts. I can stand only five minutes outside to check out this beautiful setting, and I have seen enough. I am flat-out gross and disgusting because of my sweat. Yuck. Sonny and I will stay here inside our van.

I realize this kvetching makes it sound like an episode of "Karen goes Kamping." I'm withering in the heat like a wimp and sound nothing like the rugged camper I so proudly say I am. I am stinky and exhausted, but I have electricity here, and that means Sonny and I have sweet, cool air. I'm building my courage to go out in the heat to walk him again, but I keep putting it off because it is still one million suffocating degrees outside.

I sit here petting my dog. There's no internet service, so I can't get on Facebook or check the news.

That was one of the big draws to hitting the road. I crave this disconnection because I've become addicted to bad news and stupid reels on social media. I am desperate for a break, but now that I'm forced to have one cold turkey, I am going through a mean withdrawal.

I want to sit and be where I am. Just sit here. But this is disorienting! I glance at my phone, then force myself to look away. This is an unsettling silence. No notifications, no breaking news alerts, just me sitting here with Sonny in this air-conditioned van.

Isn't this the best? My mind is clear! Just being here with no internet, I'm free! I'm cleansed! I'm rediscovering the art of daydreaming and the luxury of boredom. I grab a book—a real one with pages that rustle.

I'm lying.

I want internet, and I want it now. I don't feel like reading a real book.

I look at my phone, pick it up, double-check to make sure there really is no service, and keep thinking I can somehow magically reconnect. I turn it off and on twice, hoping it finds a smidge of service, but nothing. There really is none. This morning, I knew every global crisis, celebrity scandal, and dog meme. Now I am ignorant of such things and can only sit here pondering nothing. I'm going to get used to this. I vow I will.

I have longed to disconnect, but here in this heat, I feel it would be helpful to at least know what the royal family is doing.

There will be many, many times when there is zero service in the wilds where I will travel. I have to make peace with this.

I'm dying to know if anybody has texted or emailed.

I can't even call anybody to complain about the fact that I can't call them.

Sonny and I sit here doing nothing.

No news. No politicians saying inflammatory things that upset me. No wars. No hate.

If I don't read it or see it, does it exist? Seriously, I'm asking. If I don't know about something, am I ignorant or enlightened?

Because as uncomfortable as it is not to know, it's a relief.

WANDER WOMAN

I am at a stoplight in Arlington, Texas when a woman signals for me to roll down my window.

"Do you drive in that or live in it?" she asks.

"I've just started my first big trip!" I say enthusiastically.

"You're going by yourself?"

"Well, I have him," I say, proudly pointing at Sonny, who is peering out the side window.

"I want to do that so badly," she says. "I'm afraid to do it."

To her, I am one hell of a lot cooler than I actually am.

I've always been fascinated by people who cut out and leave their routines, ever since a reporter I worked with at *The Miami Herald* ran away with her lover to live in a Paris apartment across from the Eiffel Tower, leaving her husband behind. A few years later, my friend Jill and her then-boyfriend left demanding jobs as forensic pathologists and spent a year traveling around the world. My friend Anne and her husband packed their sailboat and hit the high seas. I always asked why I didn't have the guts to do it.

My ex-husband Geoff and I were in Greece when he gave me the answer. We met two American women teaching English abroad. They were living on the island of Santorini and told us about their big adventure as we watched the sun set into the Aegean Sea.

"Why don't we do something like that?" I asked Geoff.

"Because we're Jewish and our mothers would kill us," he answered flatly.

We laughed, but it was so true. We were raised to grow up, have good careers, contribute to society, and take vacations every now and again. Most people live like that. The more you do it, the more money you likely will be paid, which helps you to improve your standard of living, which keeps you trapped. You can afford nice homes and nice things, and you'd like to keep them.

Work more, live less.

Or…

Work less, live more!

I started really thinking about the power of downsizing in 2008 when the Great Recession loomed. I knew companies weren't going to be hiring many high-priced motivational speakers for expensive conferences when they were laying off tens of thousands of employees at a time. I found comfort in looking at a sailboat anchored offshore from the path I walked every morning.

"I can just do that!" I would tell myself. Like Fawn Germer would actually sell her house and buy a little sailboat and live on it, moored offshore.

I was fascinated by the bearded man I often saw reading on deck. He wasn't paying rent, electricity, water bills, yard service, pool service, housekeeping, gas, or any of the other regular bills I was paying. He'd row his dinghy ashore if he needed to do errands or wanted to walk or mingle.

I finally met him. James was a 52-year-old former pharmaceutical rep who said his divorce left him broke and in a mid-life crisis. He sold his car, bought a sailboat for $6,000, and lived on the waterfront.

"What a dream life," I said wistfully.

"Don't get sucked into the romance of this," he said. "This is actually just a step up from living in your car."

He talked about living with zero room, dealing with bad weather, and the endless list of things breaking onboard.

"Do you get bored?"

"Every day," he said. "It's very lonely."

"What is the advantage?"

"Few bills, I don't have a job, and I don't get stressed."

He said he was living on less than $500 a month from what was left in his retirement fund.

So much for my fantasy of packing up and heading out to sea. It's good that my business actually went up during the recession because I'd quickly published *Finding the Up in the Downturn*, a book that showed how to create success in the face of economic challenges.

I was damn lucky not to have to live in a little sailboat, and I never forgot what I learned from James. What might seem like an idyllic way of life may actually be the opposite.

Ten years after I fantasized about living on a sailboat, someone told me about the "Gone with the Wynns" channel on YouTube. It was a cute, young couple who traveled in their RV, then sold it and bought a sailboat and sailed the world. Jason and Nikki Wynns are photographers, filmmakers, and storytellers, and they made me want to be just like them. I wanted to wake up and, on a whim, go scuba diving with whales or paddle boarding in a glacier field. I found other channels that showed the wonders of their freedom. I followed vanlifers on Facebook.

Freedom called me.

But I always remembered James.

Those of us who dare to get up and go will discover and define the truth of this kind of experience for ourselves. I don't know what I'm going to bring home from this. That woman at the traffic light sees me as somebody courageous, lucky, and marvelous just because I'm driving in a van with my dog. This *is* a magical experience. But she is looking at me in the same way I looked at James out there, reading books on his sailboat offshore in Clearwater.

I am lighter and more energized than I have been in years. I hope that will last.

I was afraid to do this. I was afraid to spend the money on the van, afraid to ditch my career for an extended period, afraid to leave my home unattended, afraid it would cost way more than it seemed, afraid I would get hurt, afraid that there were too many unknowns.

But isn't it weird how none of that fear exists now that I've left? I'm in charge of me now.

I am excited about the rest of my life, not resigned to it. I don't know what I'm going to be when I grow up, and I'm good with that. I'll figure it out, or not, living as I go.

I cried when I got to Michelle's home in Arlington. I'd made it across country. My reward was time with one of my life soulmates.

I look at my life's achievements, and this is definitely up there. The achievement is not driving from home to Michelle's house in Texas. It was deciding not to delay doing what I wanted to do. It was facing my fears and leaving the driveway.

I stood in her kitchen, and we hugged, tight. So tight. And then I hugged her again. And a few minutes later, again, because I am so lucky for this friendship.

Plus, I'm proud. I left. I did.

I left.

I still hear Geoff explaining why we couldn't take off and do things like this. Our mothers would have killed us.

But now that I've done it, I feel very close to my late mother.

I can almost hear her cheering, "You can do it!"

BAD HAIR DAYS

The decision to stop coloring my hair came about because white hair is in, as is good gray. My hair grows so fast that I dye it at least every three weeks. That's a lot of chemicals, and I want to stop the insanity of this cycle. I stopped coloring it four weeks before I left.

So far, it's a big yuck. My roots are so noticeable, and I feel older every time I look in the mirror.

I was warned about this, so I try not to look.

This is the price of seeing what I look like without color. "Won't it be great when I don't have to color my hair anymore?" I say that over and over again, but I realize I'm trying to talk myself into something.

I have never had the patience to go to a salon and waste a whole afternoon of my time and hundreds of my dollars to get my color just right. It's been me and Nice'n Easy 6 forever. I have that drill down, but I'm sick of it. I have so much gray, color-resistant hair that I leave that blob of dye on my hair for almost an hour. That cannot be good. If ever there's a time to go natural, this is it. I am not going to color my hair in a campground shower. I'm going to suck it up and do this.

When I look in the mirror, my hair looks mousy, and it brings out my wrinkles. The colored part is getting lighter, and the gray part looks haggard. For this reason, I am almost always wearing a hat these days.

I got a short haircut two weeks ago and will get a couple of cuts down the road. I wear a baseball cap as much as possible, but there's no hiding what's going on. It looks like I've let myself go. My pictures look ridiculous—and they are looking worse every day—but I have committed to doing this. I am going to see what I look like with gray hair.

Today was a C- bad hair day. I want to enjoy it because we are days away from being in the D+ zone.

THE GOLDEN GIRLS

"Are you best friends?" a young associate asks Michelle, Karin, and me. This occurs after 11 p.m. on a dessert run to Walmart. "You all remind me of the Golden Girls!"

I feign being very insulted, but maybe I am a little insulted. I see us as Monica, Rachel, and Phoebe on *Friends*, but she sees us as Rose, Dorothy, and Blanche on the old lady show.

It *is* really funny. But I still wonder how all of this happened so fast. How did we get to be "old" when we were the young ones just a little while ago? When I was 22, I viewed my 31-year-old coworker, Evelyn, as an all-knowing, responsible, and wise woman. My boss, Nick, was also 31, but he seemed like he was fifty-something—like my dad. The old guy who sat across from me was 36. One ancient female reporter was only 45.

They were the grownups in the room. They'd already figured out how to handle life and deal with mortgages and long-term relationships. They carried themselves with authority and looked more tired, busy, and stressed by life—especially if they had kids. I was hired in 1983 with a group of other young journalists, mostly 24- to 26-year-olds, and we socialized among ourselves because we didn't know what we didn't know, and we liked it that way. We were the free, curious, and adventurous ones who partied until 4 a.m. and were back at work five hours later. I'm sure some of the "old people" in their early 30s judged us as being young, naïve, and reckless when they went home to houses and responsibilities, all grown up.

But looking back, we were all just a bunch of kids.

I do this every now and again. I think of people who seemed old to me when I was young, then look up their birth year and do the math to find out how very young they were. When I do that, I can accept that young people like the woman in Walmart see me as old.

What I'm having trouble accepting is that I now see it when I look at myself. I fought it off for years with Botox and fillers because I was competing for keynotes in a superficial industry that celebrates the young and ignores the old. But I am sick of doing that, just like I'm sick of coloring my hair. I would love to look young and not need any touch-ups, but I have reached the point where a touch-up isn't enough, and I'm not willing to do anything drastic.

So, whatever. Love thyself. I'm working on it.

I went to dinner with seven friends in Texas tonight. We hadn't seen each other in seven years, which doesn't feel like a long time, but we all looked different—and we all tried to look like we weren't looking at each other. It was a delicate dance of glances, and I know I wasn't judging them, but I was wondering what they were thinking about me.

A few minutes in, we started laughing, and the mood was electric.

My heart hurt when my friend Ajax showed up riding a mobility scooter. He is one of my biggest cheerleaders and a member of my Texas posse. It had been six years since I'd seen him, and his multiple sclerosis is progressing. He and his wife, Barb, are so madly in love, in sickness and in health. They celebrate anniversaries every week and every month. He has so much to face, yet he is a joyful man—and that makes me stop thinking about my wrinkles and focus instead on gratitude for my health.

When we got home tonight, Karin and I talked about how Barb and Ajax have such an amazing love. We pondered what we would do with something like that. What do we actually want, now that we have both found ourselves single at this age?

It feels like some married friends feel sorry for us because we haven't found "the one." Well, I have found "the one" several times and now know that "the one" is my dog. At least, for now.

Is there a problem with that?

Karin and I talk about how it might not be bad (look at how I worded that) to have somebody in our lives, sorta, maybe. But not living with us, checking in every day, having expectations, trying to control us or take our space.

Being single is so fulfilling. And you can ask my former partner, because we still see each other all the time. But after about 90 minutes, we know somebody needs to go home. We love being solo.

I wonder if this is a new want for women. Mine is a trailblazing generation that has choices that our mothers and grandmothers didn't. We know how to say no. Karin and I think it would be great to have a partner or someone to love who lives next door or a few miles away, who comes and goes—some of the time. I know a lot of people will judge our definition of a relationship as inferior to the traditional model, but we think it sounds just great.

One of my friends got a call this week, and I heard her husband on the other end of the phone saying, "Just checking on you."

I don't want to be checked on. At this point, I don't want to get permission for anything. I want to be the one who has to give it.

A DESPERATE ODYSSEY

After a long, hot, boring drive through the expansive nothingness of northern Texas, I have an encounter with fear and desperation. I booked a place to camp through Harvest Host, an online RV member-ship site that matches campers with farms, wineries, breweries, and other attractions where they can stay the night in exchange for supporting the businesses.

I head to the Route 66 Welcome Center in Amarillo, Texas, which looks like a really cool place in the listing, but I get nervous when I see it is in an industrial part of town.

It still seems cool until the manager says, "You're our only camper tonight."

Oh, hell no.

Roadside wonders on Route 66 in Amarillo

Amarillo Texas

There is no way I am camping there by myself, parked in a corner in an industrial area that my crime app reports has had violent assaults and a shooting in recent weeks.

I've been told to listen to my gut, and my gut says no, no, no, no, no.

I leave.

A great alternative, I think, will be to camp at Palo Duro Canyon State Park, about 45 minutes away. I want to see the canyon anyhow. Since they don't offer same-day reservations online, I drive there.

"We don't take reservations here," the ranger says. "All reservations have to be done online."

"But I can't do it online," I say, pleading. "It can't be done on the same day. I need a spot now."

He shrugs. They have *dozens* of available campsites, but he either can't or won't help me, despite my begging.

It's after 4 p.m., my GPS has lost the signal, and I am nervous. The sun hangs in the sky like a relentless spotlight. This is no scenic road trip. I am nowhere, where the horizon stretches to forever. My anxiety grows as my useless phone GPS searches for nonexistent satellites. This landscape is just tumbleweeds, occasional mesquite trees, and the skeletal remains of a long-dead armadillo. No gas stations, no towns, nothing. My van is a speck in this vast oven.

I'm a T-Mobile customer, but I got myself a Verizon phone for moments just like this, to cover the gaps. Verizon isn't any better.

I don't know where I am or where I'm going, but I still have plenty of gas. I really want a place to park "stealth," sleep, and regroup.

Stealth camping is what van people do when they show up in parking lots, neighborhoods, at hospitals, in apartment complexes or hotels, then put up window covers for privacy while they sleep. I practiced stealth camping before I left, in a Hampton Inn parking lot in Dunedin and a Cracker Barrel outside of Orlando. Cracker Barrel and Walmart actually *encourage* people to camp there at night, so it's not really stealth.

But in Nowhere, Texas, there is a whole lot of nothing. Few trees, no houses, no service, and certainly no Cracker Barrel. Just wide-open, exceedingly hot open space for miles and miles where my tall white

Winnebago van with my bike and gear bins on the back serve as glaring evidence that I am overnighting illegally.

I've read about getting the dreaded nighttime "knock" when the sheriff or somebody scarier pounds on the van door. If that happens, Sonny will bark like a vicious killer dog, blowing my cover. I'll answer for law enforcement, and then the officer will likely tell me to move along. I am so scared I'll have to search in the pitch black of night to find my way back to a GPS signal where I might find my way to civilization. But what if the person knocking on the van is a serial killer (and please note I always worry about serial killers, not just regular killers)? Nobody on YouTube or in the forums has a great answer for that.

It's getting later when I see a brewery in the middle of this expanse. I am elated and so hopeful when I ask the manager if I can camp in the parking lot overnight.

"No," she says, quick and firm.

Lesson learned. Never ask. But I doubt I would have gotten away with it if I'd done it without asking.

I have no idea where I am going to stay.

Ugh. I worried about this kind of thing before I left. I'm stressed, but now that I'm in the air conditioning at this brewery, I remember that when the universe can't be forced, I should stop trying to force it.

I am concerned, yes, a little afraid, sure, and anxious. But I have my van, my bed, and my dog. I have a ton of food and water. I'll live.

"Let it go," I tell myself. "Leave it for a minute."

I cool off, order a deliciously cold beer, and watch Sonny work the crowd there.

"Can I pet your dog?" everybody asks.

"Of course," I answer, holding back from saying, "Can I sleep in your driveway?"

I have never stopped for a beer like this. But this is a very good beer, and I have stopped freaking out.

Suddenly, my phone works. There is Wi-Fi! I reconnect with GPS. I call my friend Cathy, who I'm hoping to see while in the area.

As soon as I talk to her, everything gets so easy.

Cathy tells me to meet her in Canyon, Texas, which isn't far away.

Arriving in Canyon is like arriving in van heaven. I see a Hampton Inn, a Holiday Inn Express, and a Best Western. I have my choice of parking lots for the night! I have dinner with Cathy and her husband, then sleep in the lot at the Hampton.

I've beaten back the panic. I also know that the next time I freak out about not having a place to stay, it will be easier. I've lived through it once, and I did just fine.

After eight hours of perfect sleep, I drive back to Palo Duro Canyon for sunrise. It's overcast and definitely doesn't show off the panoramic magic of the canyon I've seen in photos, but something special happens. Sonny meets the West.

Sonny checking out the expanse of Palo Duro Canyon.

My little Florida boy knows beaches, woods, and small mountains. But when he sees that canyon, he is mesmerized. Little Man climbs on a ledge and stares at the expanse for several minutes as his world transforms. That vastness defies his understanding. What is this bottomless pit? A gateway to other worlds?

His tail wags, uncertain but curious. What is he thinking? Because he sure looks deep in thought. Or maybe it's one giant "Wowwwww." I wish I knew. He experiences nature in such a human way. He stops to watch sunrises and sunsets. I have never seen a dog more captivated by God's Greatest Hits.

He does the same three-mile hike in the woods every day at home, at least once, but often twice a day.

Now he will wake up to mountains, canyons, waterfalls, lakes, and new people. He'll explore trails and stores and campgrounds and people's homes.

I am trying to look at life like he does. He's my teacher. The way he takes in the moment makes *me* live in the moment.

Little Man and I are leaving our ruts.

ABQ

I need a shower. Badly. It's been about 30 hours, and driving, gas stations, high heat, and camping in a hotel parking lot can stink a person up. Finally, Sonny and I arrive at Kyla Thompson's house in Albuquerque, New Mexico. Her home has towering ceilings, exposed wood beams, exquisite hardwood floors, and wood furnishings carved by her husband, Roger.

Enter Sonny Germer, who charges in like the Merrill Lynch bull, racing past his hostess to inspect every room, moving so fast that nobody can apprehend him. "Stop!" I yell, but he ignores me. Kyla knows Sonny through Facebook, so fortunately, she already loves him before he jumps on her furniture, showing their poor 10-year-old Lab, Desi, that he is now in charge. This is Sonny's worst behavior, ever. He is delighted to be liberated from the tight quarters of the van. Fortunately, Kyla and Roger are dog people with huge, understanding hearts and quality furniture that can withstand his antics.

"It was an invasion," Kyla says with a laugh.

After lunch, Kyla hands me a towel and tells me to enjoy a shower. I am learning that my friends are more than happy to let me clean up, wash clothes, or even plug in and stay in the driveway for the night.

I step into that hot shower, the first droplets reminding me of my simplest pleasure of life—warm water making me clean.

I head next to catch up with an old ex and her wife who also live in Albuquerque. Two of my friends warned me it was a huge mistake to revisit that particular relationship, but we were so young back then. I have stayed friends with almost every person I have ever been with. What is the risk of saying hello to someone left in my long-ago past?

La, la, la. Tra, la, laa. People come into our lives—sometimes relationships work, sometimes they don't. But they all add up to a life, right?

Well…

Nearly 30 years later, I learn that there are some relationships that should be left in the past. Not every loose end needs to be tied up. This is not enjoyable, she is not being kind, and when I have had enough, I say goodbye and leave.

I get in my van and drive away with my dog, feeling so powerful because I see how I have grown after all of these years.

But I am never, ever, *ever* doing that again.

LET'S HIKE

Twenty minutes from gorgeous Taos, New Mexico, I detour down a steep dirt road, put on my hiking boots, and hit the trail with Sonny. Because I need to be at a friend's house in Salida, Colorado tonight, my choice is to hike or do Taos, not both.

I'm not going to worry about towns and cities on this trip. I wasted yesterday in Santa Fe because every sensible New Mexico visitor goes there and I figured I should, too.

Our first hike. My heart is soaring.

But I'm here to adventure and experience. I want to hike, bike, kayak, and see friends.

My trip, my way.

I have been itching for an answer on whether I will be able to hike on my bad knee. This impromptu course-change is a three-mile steady uphill trail with varied rock formations and steep drop-offs. It's fairly wide and mostly simple, but it's the kind of thing that my orthopedic surgeon warned me to avoid. If it bothers my knee, I promise myself I will turn around. I don't want to hurt myself, but I also don't want to miss anything.

I tighten my brace and tell myself, "Don't be foolish."

I have been telling myself that since I was in my 20s. It's a version of "Do everything possible, but don't be stupid."

Today, I *really* feel like hiking.

It isn't hard, and what a thrill to walk my boy in that dusty landscape in front of me. It's so quiet!

I feel strong. My knee is working! Sonny cannot believe his good fortune out here. His eager paws are practically dancing on the trail, and he has to stop to smell *everything*. He isn't hiking Hammock Park. He is hiking a big, new world. He's got a wild heart, that boy.

TWENTY-SIX YEARS LATER

I am in Colorado now, on my friend Tara's property with a view of the expanse of the Sawatch Mountains and the Collegiate Peaks. This is one of the best views in Colorado, and she lives here.

Coming back is so emotional.

As I boarded a direct flight from Denver to Tampa and moved home to Florida, I said these words: "As God is my witness, I will never be cold again." That was July 1997. I meant it, but I have never stopped thinking about Colorado. I have come back for visits over and over again, but never for more than a week at a time.

My time here, from age 29 to 37, had been such a mix for me. Emotionally, I was in chaos. I had my feminist awakening, started fighting for battered women, had the world's worst bosshole, divorced, started dating women, and was the last person anyone would have trusted to write the self-help books that have become my trademark. I lacked the confidence that I have now, and I experienced moments of very low self-esteem.

Those times were as exciting, rewarding, and uplifting as they were emotionally challenging. While I struggled to find out who I was, I was also doing my best work as a journalist and was physically stronger than I'd ever been. I had the best friends. I laughed so hard and had so much fun.

I cycled, skied downhill and cross-country, snowshoed, hiked, and breathed in those mountains every single day, whether I was up in them or looking at them from down in Denver. They were the best times, but they were such a struggle.

I wanted a new job because of my bosshole, but I only looked for employment back home on the West Coast of Florida so I could be near my mom and dad. I constantly worried about my mom after her stroke, and I faithfully flew home several times a year. But being a drive-by daughter didn't work for me. This was the best and most important decision of my life because I had 15 years of weekly visits and intimate moments with my beloved parents.

And I was home.

The minute I moved back to Florida, I was in my skin again. Maybe it was being near my mom and dad or the elixirs of big water and warm weather, which let my soul breathe, but the difficulties of my eight years in Colorado dissolved when my plane landed in Tampa. It was the damnedest thing.

The other damnedest thing was that I never let go of Colorado, even after all those years. Twenty-six years have passed, and I think about Colorado every day. It's inside of me.

Crossing the border today feels like I am coming home after being gone a month or so.

Twenty-six years.

And here I am. Approaching the border, I play my Spotify playlist that includes everything that was on my old Sony Walkman when I cycled mountain passes back in my 30s: The Rolling Stones, The

Eagles, Johnny Clegg, Tina Turner, Madonna, Aretha Franklin, Heart, Bruce Hornsby, Peter Gabriel, Motown Classics, The Pretenders, Eurythmics—I am in the Wayback Machine.

Back then, cycling was my life. I was obsessed with it—cycled so many century rides and on a few occasions rode more than 200 mountain miles in a day.

Where is that woman? I wonder. While I was so strong physically, I struggled with my identity. I was newly divorced, finding my way out of daily journalism, coming out of the closet, and dealing with my beloved mother becoming paralyzed—all at once.

And here I am, back in Colorado and again in an identity crisis.

Did I just admit that?

Yeah, that is a fact. I love my 60s, but I don't love what others ascribe to women in their 60s. I am sorting my feelings.

I don't want to have the "invisible woman syndrome," but there are times when I feel dismissed and invisible. This is not whining. There are so many studies on this. Society stops noticing and valuing middle-aged and late-middle-aged women, and that has impacted my career as a mainstage keynote speaker.

I'm not a has-been. I'm still right here. I'm right here inside of me. That woman who used to cycle up those hard mountain passes is still in here, I know it, but I can't access her. The woman who fought her way onto the best-seller lists? Still here. Traveled the globe keynoting for Fortune 500 companies? She's still in here.

But I don't feel noticed or heard. I feel more invisible than invincible.

I want to change that while I can still see myself.

I want to see how we can all come into our power again, not as cliché feisty old ladies like Maxine on Hallmark cards, but as the powerhouses who earned the respect we still deserve.

I want to think about it, but I also don't. This stuff hurts.

DEAN

A pickup truck apparently doesn't like how slow I'm going as I drive over Cottonwood Pass, so the driver starts honking. I guess my going the speed limit is ruining their day, but I am enjoying the snow around me on the Continental Divide. The truck passes me, then slows down about 10 mph below the speed limit. The passenger lowers his window, sticks his arm out, and flips me off. Then the driver lowers his window and also flips me off. They honk again, then speed off.

What has happened to people? What is there to be angry about at 12,126 feet of elevation, surrounded by magical, snow-covered Rocky Mountain peaks?

Apparently, it's a crime that I am not in a rush.

There is no oncoming traffic. Why didn't they just pass me if they didn't like me going the speed limit? Everything doesn't have to require conflict and rage. But this irks me because I see it all the time. Not just on the road. Everybody is so ready to blow up.

But they have to get around me, slow down, and flip me off before they can head off at their chosen speed, which is no more than 5 mph faster than I am going. Fifteen minutes pass, and they are still right in front of me. What was the point?

I see a pull-off and stop to eat lunch next to a rushing creek. That's the beauty of traveling in the van. I pull over somewhere great, open the fridge, sit on my couch with Sonny, and enjoy lunch in front of a million-dollar view. Lunch probably cost me less than a dollar, but it is priceless.

I'm so excited because I'll soon be with Dean Krakel, my guru and man crush.

Dean and I worked together at the now-shuttered *Rocky Mountain News* when I was a reporter and he was a photographer and editor. We stayed close because he is like me: He values time over money and adventure over career. Several years ago, he took a buyout as photo editor at *The Denver Post* so he could hike the 566-mile Colorado Trail. There is an inspiring documentary about him doing it. The next year, he spent five months on the hardest hike, the Continental Divide Trail. Ever since, it has been an endless adventure for him. His Facebook page is a constant call to live.

But.

With Dean, just three weeks after his stroke

Three weeks ago, at age 70, Dean suffered a stroke. He is fighting his way back.

It is sobering to see him weakened. How is this possible? Dean is Superman. But today, he's not his old self—and he knows that. He also knows that, after what he has been through, he never will be again, if just psychologically.

He describes what he went through at the hospital: "All these faces were looking down at me, and I couldn't move my arm," he says. "I thought to myself, *I could die here*. Then I thought, *No fucking way. I'm not going*."

We are in his living room when Dean looks out his window and points at a mountain behind his home. Not long ago, he raced up that mountain in under 30 minutes. It's one and a half miles up and 719 feet of vertical gain. That is *steep*. As he aged, he was glad he could still do it in under 40 minutes. Just before the stroke, he was trying to beat an hour, which is still better than 99.999 percent of the population.

But today, he can't do it at all.

He's confronting limits, as we all are.

But he's also blasting past them. He's already gone hiking and paddle boarding, but he wears out. He'll be biking soon, and I know he'll be skiing once the snow comes.

But he knows he's likely to have stroke-related problems for the rest of his life.

We have a deep conversation about coming to grips with aging. We are not who we were. We cannot do what we did. Dean is trying to make peace with it, but I am in denial. I think that somewhere inside me lives that extreme cyclist who can bike up any mountain with ease and ride hundreds of miles in a day. My van struggles to drive those same roads, and I wonder how the hell I did any of that, over and over, every week, hundreds of miles at a time.

Dean stops me from going into a mental loop as I lament my loss of strength.

"You can't compare yourself to yourself. Not yourself 30 years ago, not yourself 10 years ago, and not even yourself last year. You can't compete against others. Or young people. You can just do what you can do today."

It doesn't make me feel better, but it does help me see a path toward coping. I still want to be Fawn, the athlete. Fawn, the adventurer. Fawn, the unstoppable.

But I am not. And that pisses me off.

I want to be able to do what I used to do. We all do, don't we? It doesn't feel good to have to slow down, and I'm wrestling with the notion.

Do we really have to? I know there comes a point when there is no choice about it, but I look at a lot of my friends in their sixties, and they've let themselves slide into a life of inertia. They stop moving.

When you stop moving, you can't move.

When you stop thinking, you can't think.

When you stop, you stop.

Health challenges come with the territory. I saw that with my mom. But a lot of healthy people slip into poor health because they give up the fight.

We are fighting for our lives.

The less we do, the less we can do. For the body to work, it needs to be put to work.

That's why this is so frustrating for Dean. He's got the fight in him. He wants to work his body and work his mind, but the stroke took charge. Now it's a daily battle. It's hit his psyche, and he knows he is not invincible.

But let me tell you this: He is still Dean Krakel, and my money is on him.

DOWNTIME

Twelve days in, and I have no clue what day it is.

And the date? I have to look it up every time. Twelve days in, and I have learned to be where I am, doing what I want. I'm even getting used to spotty or no internet service.

I love when I don't know what is going on in the world.

I feel relieved to find things out later, if at all.

You know what Sonny and I are doing today? Nothing. Well, I gave him a bath this morning, and he is now twice as dirty as he was before the bath because he keeps rolling in the dirt. But we need a down day, so I am sitting in a $12 Walmart camping chair under a tree. Sitting and writing. And thinking. But not thinking hard.

It's time I face something I don't want to face: my dirty laundry.

It's a privilege to sit here in the Rockies, where my biggest problem is dirty laundry.

Peace of mind and peace of heart are so much easier to come by than we realize when we're caught up in the chaos of life. We get so trapped in our heads, worrying about things that won't happen or things that don't matter. But if we can stop for a minute and sit still, we can experience delicious moments of peace. We don't have to drive thousands of miles to find this. We all have chairs.

WHO I WAS VS. WHO I AM

I divorced the man I loved in 1993. Geoff and I still loved each other, but he wanted to change jobs and move to a new state on another side of the country every year, and I didn't. Both of our hearts broke when our marriage unraveled.

It was too much to process.

I avoided it by becoming even more passionate about cycling. I was no longer satisfied with biking more than 225 miles a week. One Saturday, I biked up the brutal Independence Pass outside Aspen, climbing 4,000 feet to 12,095 feet, and I didn't feel like I'd had enough of a workout. I raced back down, then climbed the whole thing again. Sane people don't do that. I was unstoppable because I knew that if I stopped, I'd have to think about what was going on in my life.

I was coming undone. This is a long but important story from my life and has everything to do with why I am here and what is nagging at me now.

It's funny how my avoidance worked back then. I started doing double centuries in the mountains, something few ever tried. A double century is 200 miles of cycling—in a day—and I always went farther than that. I signed up to do something called the Death Ride, a barbaric circuit that began and ended in Durango, which only a handful of men and one woman had done at that time.

The Death Ride covered 230 miles over seven mountain passes with 21,000 feet of elevation gain. It's one of the most celebrated scenic mountain drives in the United States, and it's exhausting to do it in a car.

I was sure I could do it on my bicycle, but the guys in the bike club weren't. I'd already done a double century with them the previous year. But these guys did not think I could do the Death Ride—and told me so before I left.

"You have no idea what you're getting into and, while we can't stop you, you need to reconsider this," said the man in charge of the ride, which was sponsored by my cycling club.

I assured him I was up to it, as I had already done 210 miles in one day—over Trail Ridge Road in Rocky Mountain National Park, which is the highest continuous road in the United States. Yet the man said, "You should not be doing this."

I didn't agree.

I asked my next-door neighbor, Joe, to go with me and check on me in the afternoon.

The experience was one of the most profound lessons in life I've ever had. It's a story about a bike ride, but it's a more important story about staring down adversity.

My plan was to start with the boys in the parking lot of the Durango Holiday Inn. I would treat my ride as if it were a normal training ride for the first 160 miles. Instead of acknowledging the difficulty or my exhaustion, I'd just tell myself it was a no-big-deal training ride. At mile 120, when I reached the top of Lizard Head Pass, I would be rewarded with a 40-mile downhill, which I would use to recover. Then, with the worst 160 miles behind me, I would allow myself to acknowledge I was on the Death Ride doing something super-human (for me) for the final 70 miles.

Me at age 30, having just climbed the Molas Divide. I was obsessed with endurance cycling for the eight years that I lived in Colorado.

My mantra was, "This is nothing until mile 160."

I started riding with four men at 1:30 a.m. The plan was for Joe to catch up with me around 3 p.m. outside Telluride. The guys immediately left me in their dust.

But I had a secret weapon: a cassette tape with all of my favorite tunes on it, including the Rolling Stones, Tina Turner, Madonna, Heart, Springsteen, The Spinners, Johnny Clegg, Peter Gabriel, and the like. Between each song, I had the voices of my friends and family telling me that they knew I could do it. Even Geoff, my ex-husband, was on the tape.

Your friends and family will get you there.

I pedaled through Durango and up that first pass, Coal Bank Pass, in the black of night with my little battery-operated light on the front of my bike. I listened to my favorite music and the people I loved most telling me I was not alone.

It didn't matter that Coal Bank Pass was hard. It didn't even count in my mind. Nothing would count in my mind until that last 70 miles.

I summited the second pass, the Molas Divide, at sunrise. *Mustang Sally* played on my Walkman and the water guy from the bike club was waiting when I got there. I'd paid $80 just to get water every 15 to 20 miles, which was a huge amount of money for water in 1993, but well worth it.

I sped down the pass into Silverton over the Million Dollar Highway, then climbed Red Mountain Pass and onward to the town of Ouray. Even for the best cyclists, that was already a full day of riding, but I had so far to go, and I kept telling myself, "This is nothing until mile 160."

I rode through Ouray, over to Ridgeway, then crossed the Dallas Divide. I felt strong and had so much music with me that I was fully entertained as I started to close in on Lizard Head Pass.

But before I got to Lizard Head, I was in a full-on crisis.

As I descended the Dallas Divide, I realized my water supply was down to about an inch of water in my bottle. It was about 1 p.m., and I had not seen the water guy since the top of Molas Pass, so it had been several hours and more than 50 painful mountainous miles.

I was dragging, dehydrated, and about to bonk.

I didn't know what to do.

I was in the middle of *nowhere*. Miles away from water or convenience stores or signs of humanity. This was pre-cell phone, and it was just me, my bike, and the cassettes on my Walkman.

"Just keep pedaling," I told myself. When I don't know what to do in life, I try to just keep moving forward, whether it has to do with my bike or my work or anything else.

I kept pedaling. I was out of water, it was hot, and I knew the time was near when I'd have to stop. But how do you quit in a situation like that? There was no air-conditioned store or house where I could stop and say, "I give up."

"Just keep pedaling," I said. "Keep moving forward. Just keep pedaling." I said it over and over.

Suddenly, I heard a horn honking repeatedly behind me.

I looked in the rearview cycling mirror clipped to my sunglasses.

"Bee-bee-bee-bee-beeep!!!!"

It was Joe! And he was early! He pulled over, and I asked, "Do you have water?"

"I have water, I have Gatorade, I have food. What do you need?" he said.

"Don't lose me," I told him.

I am crying as I write this. It remains one of the most memorable moments of deep friendship I have experienced. I was back in the game.

I drank until I felt hydrated, then filled my bottles and headed toward the top of Lizard Head Pass. I was about to reach mile 120, the most critical moment of the ride. The other side of that pass would be that 40-mile gradual descent to take me to mile 160.

But guess who was up there when I summited?

Yep. The water guy.

"You're going too slow," he said. "I'm going to put you in the truck and move you forward because I can't keep coming back for you."

Well, I don't know about you, but after riding 120 miles in the heat with no water, I was not to be trifled with.

"Look," I said, "the rule was I had to do this within 24 hours, *which I will do.* I paid $80 so you could bring me water, so you need to bring me water. I'm not getting in your truck."

"You have to," he said.

"I don't," I said.

"I can't come back for you. You're too far behind the men. You have to move forward."

"No, I don't."

There is always, always someone telling you that you are doing it wrong and you need to quit. Do not listen to that voice.

"Get in the truck," he insisted.

"No," I said firmly.

At that moment, dear Joe pulled in behind me.

"How's it going?" he asked cheerily.

I was so happy to see him.

"Will you follow me and make sure I have water and everything I need?" I asked.

"Oh yeah," he said.

"Bye-bye," I said to the water guy, waving him off.

I started down Lizard Head Pass, ready to enjoy that glorious 40-mile gradual descent I'd been waiting on all day.

Surprise.

I ran right into the worst headwind I'd ever experienced.

I didn't get the expected 40-mile gradual descent that would let me recover from all of the day's challenges. I had to pedal down the mountain. Hard.

Just when you expect things to get easier, they are going to get harder. Keep moving forward.

Joe was waiting with water along the way, and 50 miles on the other side of the pass, he laid out a picnic next to a stream. When I stopped for that picnic, I actually sat down to rest. It was the first time I'd sat down in 170 miles of cycling.

I remember blueberry muffins.

I had to get moving again, but I had a big problem: When I tried to stand, I could not do it. I couldn't get myself up.

I remember Joe stretching his arms toward me and pulling me up into a stand. With great effort, I managed to get back in my bike saddle and start pedaling again. Joe and I knew in that moment that if I stopped riding, it would be over.

Off I went. Joe stood at the side of the road waiting for me every one or two miles.

"You can do it!" he'd shout. "Go, Fawn!"

I kept pedaling. I had two more passes to climb, and they were small: Mancos and Hesperus. They were so short and wouldn't have been remotely challenging on a normal day. But this wasn't normal.

The sun set as I headed up the Mancos Divide, and I was running out of gas. My legs desperately wanted to stop. But that was when I remembered my secret weapon: the tape. I loaded that cassette and heard the voices of everyone I loved cheering me on.

Mom: "I know you can do it!"

Betsy: "None of us can do it. If anyone can do it, it's you."

Daddy: "I believe in you!"

Then came Joyce and Jeanne and Diane and even Geoff. I had 90 minutes of great tunes interspersed with the voices of about 20 of my loved ones. I don't remember the details of riding those 90 minutes, but I remember my people getting me up that pass.

Your friends and family will get you there.

I had only one pass left. It was dark, and Joe drove slowly behind me with the car lights and flashers on. I felt guarded and protected. Then I started to hallucinate. I knew I was hallucinating because I was an educated person and knew that dinosaurs are extinct, but I thought I saw one at the side of the road.

"Keep moving forward!" I yelled to myself.

I kept pushing up that mountain, going so slow, but still moving forward. Finally, finally! I reached the top of the Hesperus Divide. I knew I would finish the Death Ride because the road down into Durango had a 10 percent grade. No headwind would stop that descent. My only fear was the road condition, which was not good. There were so many deep potholes on the way down, but Joe solved that problem, flashing his brights to warn me.

The descent was a screaming fast downhill, but I tried to keep myself moving as slowly as possible. I knew I wasn't mentally aware enough to control my bike at speeds of 55 mph or more, which I usually traveled on downhills. I feathered the brakes on and off so my tires wouldn't blow, and I squeezed hard so I was only going about 25 mph, which was still too fast for my state of mind. The sky started getting lighter from city lights, and I knew I was closing in on Durango.

"Just a little more," I told myself. "You've done it. A few more miles."

The road snaked left and right and left and right and then, suddenly, there it was.

Durango.

I'd done it. *I'd done it!*

I stayed focused on my safety as I coasted down the last stretch of mountain and into the parking lot of the Holiday Inn, where I'd started 19 hours earlier.

Joe was right behind me.

And guess what I saw right there in that parking lot? Yep. The guys. They were in their bike clothes, all sweated up.

"We wanted to cheer you in," one of the guys said.

But I knew better. They'd just arrived.

The tortoise had caught up to all the hares.

"Do you want to get some dinner?" another asked.

"Naw," I said. "I'm going to go with this guy."

Joe took me to Subway, and I ate a footlong BMT. I was so happy.

I did it in 19 hours and 16 minutes, and I did not ride my bike for three weeks after that.

Something that extreme is a real confidence builder. I felt powerful, which helped me process the divorce and move on. All of my goals and dreams had been built around being with Geoff, but I would make new ones.

With that history, being in this part of Colorado stirs up a lot for me.

I drive across the Dallas Divide to get to Telluride today, which is where I ran out of water on the Death Ride. Today, my van can barely make it up the 9.8 mile-haul to the top. I didn't think it was a hard pass when I cycled it three decades ago. It didn't register with me back then. But I am not strong like that now. How could I be at this age? I climbed seven of these beastly passes in 19 hours that day! Seven! My van is struggling with one!

I'm starting to feel so much respect for what I accomplished on my bike, and for who I was then. I am proud that I was that strong.

I'm not nearly as strong now, and I tell myself I don't need to be. I remember what Dean said about not comparing myself to who I was way back when or even yesterday.

But this is a constant argument in my head as I am in these mountains. I don't *need* to be that strong. But it sure would be nice to know that I could be if I wanted. And, if I'm being honest here, I want it.

I vividly remember what I looked like, felt like, and was able to do when I was 30 years younger. Where did that Fawn go? Why can't I be that strong now? It is insane to ponder this, but it bothers me. I know I'm not the only person to feel this way.

I had a hairdresser who said that "God gives and gives and gives to us, and then the day comes when God starts taking things away. It is all addition in the beginning, but then the subtraction begins."

That sounds so negative, but it's true. Maybe the challenge is to find new skills and talents to be good at when the old ones don't work for us anymore. I keep telling myself I should take up yoga, but I'm waiting for a class on yoga for impatient people. Yes, I know. I'm missing the point of yoga.

I think of who I was when I was so strong, and I remind myself that she is me. I am her. And as we all grow older, we have to stay connected to the fact that nothing erases our achievements, even if they are behind us. Whether they are physical accomplishments, familial, or even career achievements—they are still ours.

If I look in the mirror and see only the wrinkles, I miss the fact that I had the privilege of youth and aging was the price of it. I have extra wrinkles. I lived in the sun. I wish I looked as young as I feel, but I am not 33 years old and will not be 33 ever again. I had that moment and, thankfully, I lived it well.

I also have my turn to live this day, because I now have friends my age who can't. They have died or are sick. I am here, alive, and healthy.

So instead of lamenting what I can't do, I'm trying to teach myself to feel gratitude that I did it in the first place. There is new gratitude in figuring out how to fill this day with wonder.

My friend Susan told me that the founder of Kuumba Dancers and Drummers in Tampa inspired her with this lesson: "At a certain point in life, when their strength and stamina wanes, the dancers do a different dance. It is less vigorous, but far more graceful and every bit as beautiful. They don't feel diminished by this change. They feel they never could have danced in such a beautiful way when they were younger with too much energy and too little wisdom."

I am learning a new dance.

CLIMBING

You might describe what I am experiencing as a "head trip." I call it a complete mind f*ck.

It's when we believe something is impossible without even trying, and it happens when we ruminate on the negative, needlessly destroying our self-confidence.

I've been in that zone since I got to the mountains, and because of it, I haven't been able to make myself get on my bike. Isn't that why I'm here? Six days in Colorado and not one mile of cycling. Unbelievable. Watching my van struggle in the mountains convinced me that my cycling days are over. If the Ram van can barely do it, how can I? It's been years since I've cycled up anything higher than a bridge.

"If you can't do it, you can't do it," I tell myself when my alarm goes off at 6 a.m. "But you haven't even tried. Today, you try, and then you will know."

I haul myself out of bed, walk Sonny, then force myself to do what my mind-f*cked mind tells me I cannot. Today, I climb.

I slide on my Lycra shorts and a bright yellow cycling jersey, lock Sonny in the van (it's in the low 50s outside), put on my helmet, get on my road bike, and head down the mountain to the marina at Ridgeway State Park.

Did I call that a mountain? Well, it's much bigger than a hill, but as far as the Rocky Mountains go, it's minuscule. Especially for "real" cyclists. But with my mind-f*cked mind, I am not a real cyclist anymore, and this minuscule mountain is massive. I prepare for major failure trying to ride back up to the campground, knowing I'll likely poop out and have to walk it much of the way. I am grateful that Colorado is still asleep and nobody will see me struggle.

I remember the first time I rode up Lookout Mountain, a small mountain outside of Golden, Colorado where I trained after I got my first road bike in 1991. Driving up that mountain in my Honda and knowing I was about to cycle it was so intimidating! But it wasn't hard when I cycled it, and it wasn't long before that climb didn't even count as exercise.

Today, I look up at the mountain I'm about to climb, feeling as intimidated as I felt the first time I tried Lookout.

I take a deep breath, push down on the pedal with my right leg, then start heading up. Of course, I have Tina Turner singing "Steamy Windows" on my Bluetooth speaker, and then comes Patti LaBelle doing "Lady Marmalade"—and I'll be damned.

I am climbing this f*cking mountain!

Painlessly.

I'm not even slow. There's no doubt that I'll summit. I have it locked.

I can climb something!

I keep pushing—faster, faster, faster! It feels so good to push myself and feel my body respond.

By the time The Rolling Stones sing "Miss You," I am at the top, ebullient.

I turn around and celebrate by flying back downhill and doing the whole thing again.

I summit again, turn around, and go back down to the bottom.

I do it a third time!

Then a fourth!

I was so sure I would never get up to the top once!

This is not about the bike, this is not about the bike, this is *not* about the bike.

It's about telling myself I still can when I think I can't. It's about realizing I am still getting started instead of thinking I'm done. Yeah, I didn't do the Death Ride today, but I had a *great* ride.

This is not about the bike, this is not about the bike, this is *not* about the bike.

It's about the mind f*ck we play on ourselves, telling ourselves we have to settle. We don't. Or at least, we shouldn't minimize our expectations of what we can do until we try and hit the wall. Those moments will come, and we'll have to accept them with grace. But we shouldn't be afraid of the wall. If we avoid it, we will miss out on some of the greatest moments of our lives.

Back in the saddle again

The problem is doubt. I bought into that "you are past your prime" narrative, but that is a lie. I may be too old to switch careers and become a ballerina, but I'm not too old to learn ballet. There is no monopoly on success reserved for younger achievers. We don't grow if we live only in our comfort zone, but we do grow when we push it and stop embracing what is safe and predictable.

My friend Patty Ivey taught herself to play bass at age 56—by watching YouTube videos. She's 66 now and in a bunch of bands.

I have to stop comparing what I'm doing now to what I used to do and focus instead on what I am going to do next. Maybe I can't cycle 230 miles in one day anymore, but I can still cycle in the mountains. What a joy.

This makes me confront that mind f*ck. I feel so much more confident. I can't wait to cycle tomorrow because I will do it five times. I know I can. And then, when I get to Denver, I know I will be ready to train for Deer Creek Canyon so I can train for the Going to the Sun Road in Glacier National Park in Montana.

The little mountain I climbed today would have seemed like an anthill when I was young, but today, it was no anthill. It was my teacher.

I did it.

Four times.

THE TIME SONNY ALMOST SANK US

Today, we paddled.

Yes, yes, yes, we went kayaking, my favorite thing to do in life. Just me and my boy in a clear lake surrounded by high peaks.

I taught Sonny how to go kayaking soon after I rescued him. We were camping at Fort DeSoto Park in St. Petersburg, and I set the kayak out on dry land, put a doggy life vest on him, then got in the kayak. He was curious and I told him to hop in. He did, and I told him to sit, which he did. I gave him a treat. We did that about three times, and I figured we could slide the boat into the shallow water. He jumped right in, and we went paddling as if he'd done it hundreds of times.

I love kayaking with him because he loves kayaking with me. We go all the time. We go if it's a beautiful day, or if we want to take in a sunrise, sunset, or even a moonset. We go just because we feel like going. I never take him into rough water or water that might suddenly become rough. Also, no water with alligators. Sonny always wants to sit between my legs, as close as he can get to my body because he feels safer. Try operating a kayak paddle with a fifty-three-pound pit bull sitting upright between your legs. It ain't easy. If he were any closer, he'd be in my uterus. Truth.

While he loves nature, he hates dolphins, even when they're swimming far away. His body starts to shake, and he whimpers and is so frightened.

"Everything is okay," I will tell him, hugging him tight and sounding like I'm talking to a two-year-old. "Dolphins are our friends. They are a special treat from nature."

He doesn't believe me. He is also unnerved by the cormorant birds that sometimes follow us or swim under the boat. Despite those dastardly sea beasts, he still loves kayaking and is always ready to go when he sees me loading up.

Today is our virgin voyage in the Rockies, and this is very different. It's a little off-putting because the water is so cold and I don't have a sturdy kayak with me. I bought an origami kayak—made by Oru—because the van is too high for me to load one of my favorite kayaks on top. The Oru is made out of the same corrugated polypropylene plastic used for signs. It takes me six minutes to put it together and five minutes to take it apart, and it's a very good boat that folds up like a suitcase and fits inside the van, under the bed. But it doesn't feel as sturdy as what I'm used to.

Sonny is mesmerized by the scenery in Ridgeway State Park today because it's nothing like the Gulf of Mexico or a Florida river. I love watching his head move from left to right, awestruck.

There are no dolphins or cormorants to torment him, but suddenly, his head jerks to the shoreline on the left. The whimpering begins, and then the shaking.

We are at least 30 yards offshore, but Sonny starts to lunge, trying to jump out of the kayak. He's spotted big, scary, unfamiliar prey ashore, and he wants to protect Mommy.

His terror? A deer.

A big, beautiful buck stands on the shoreline, as confused by Sonny as Sonny is confused by him. Sonny wants that deer. I pull back on his collar, trying to calm him while we watch the deer watch us. I can't paddle and hold him in the boat at the same time. He keeps trying to jump out, and I am rightfully worried that Sonny will sink us because while this boat is sound, it's not made for flying dogs.

"No!" I shout. He keeps lunging as I hold his collar. "NO!"

I yell so loud this time that the buck figures it's time to bolt into the woods and get away from that crazy dog.

Sonny tries one more lunge as he sees the deer leap, but Little Man surrenders in defeat when he can no longer see the buck.

He put that thin plastic origami kayak to the test, and it passed.

I'm here, and we didn't sink—I'm just not sure how.

I CAN'T SLEEP

Why can't I sleep? I am in the most stress-free, beautiful moment of my life, yet it's 3:12 a.m., and I'm awake.

I know there is a change in front of me before I actually retire, and I'm thinking about that, waiting for the universe to tell me what I should contribute before I actually retire. Yes, I'm in this van in the woods, thinking about my career. It's time to pivot toward something, but I don't know where I'm supposed to turn.

The only reason I became a speaker was that my friend, Kerri Smith, made an offhand remark in 1999 suggesting it. I'd never even thought of this as a profession, and when I checked it out, I learned it was quite lucrative and unbelievably fun. That prompt from the universe gave me some of the greatest joy of my life. Now, I am waiting for another prompt. What am I going to do with the time I have left?

Why can't I just close my eyes and go to sleep?

By the time I turned 50, I realized that anyone who thinks they have life figured out and nailed down is either delusional or not growing.

One thing I did figure out long ago is that my purpose has nothing to do with career and everything to do with living. I know a lot of people are confused about their purpose, but I think God just wants us to live. *Really* live, and that is a powerful purpose.

I also don't think God cares one bit about our careers, influence, or money. Being kind, truthful, and purposeful matters, and we can be all of that, regardless of our positions and regardless of whether our career is on a high or a low.

A decade ago, I was in Utah and got up for sunrise at Dead Horse Point. I met Luc Parent, a Canadian man who retired early with his wife, Helene, to travel the US in their fifth-wheel trailer.

"I decided less money means more life," he said.

I put that in my phone notes and have looked at it dozens of times.

In my mind, this is what is priceless: Love. Friendship. Nature. Truth. Balance. Compassion. Forgiveness. Gratitude.

Did it matter that I was here on earth? I want to be like my dad, the kindest, most giving human being I have ever seen. He was pure love. At his funeral, the rabbi described how everyone loved and needed my father.

I often remind myself that Dad did not start out like that. When I was little and he was in his 30s, he was a good guy. By the time he was in his 50s, he was a very good guy. By the time he was in his 60s, he was a great guy. But by the time he died at 85, he had grown into a mythically great man.

My pop was a pharmacist who was still working at a pharmaceutical company until he was 84. By the end of his tenure there, he was part time and doing mostly clerical work, not filling prescriptions. But he was a larger-than-life mascot who inspired his coworkers with his positivity. His contribution had nothing to do with being a pharmacist and everything to do with being a good man.

He had to stop working after a heart attack. Dad was in a wheelchair, and I took him to his company to see his coworkers. Dozens of people lined up to see "Mr. Fred." If I'd brought in George Clooney or Brad Pitt, there would have been less response.

I want to be as good as he was, but I am not there. I don't know how I could ever get there, but I remind myself that he was always, always trying to be better.

I can do that.

I think that's why we are here. To live and love. Work is how we fill our time. We define ourselves through our humanity.

I don't have the answers to what I want to do when I grow up, but I do feel like I am winning the moment. In this moment, winning is being here, at peace. It's knowing I have everything I need. My purpose is not to need more. It's to be good and to love.

GIDDY HIGH SCHOOLERS

"We're going to crash your party," my old friend, Amy McClintock, says when I answer the phone. "We're going to camp with you this weekend."

It is on.

I am parked up at 10,500 feet in the Molas Lake Campground,

having gotten an impossible-to-get reservation for the best site I've ever had. I'm surrounded by some of the highest, snowy peaks in Colorado. Holy cow, this view!

Amy and her wife, Cindiman, show up with pizza. Good pizza. The way I've been eating on this trip (Oh, don't ask. Okay, ask. Subway. Deli meats. A few fruits and vegetables. Blech, blech, blah.), I am desperate for flavor. To me, this pizza is the best pizza in the history of pizza pie, and I'm glad they got the largest one because I take a slice, then another, then another.

We sit around the campfire, laugh, catch up, talk politics, and share the truth about what has been good and bad in our lives. We talk about old times—the ones when we were young and insecure, dealing with dramatic relationships, crappy bosses, and kooky friends. Amy and Cindiman are master rock climbers, mountain bikers, and backpackers, ultra-fit and constantly exploring and adventuring. Imagine my shock when Amy tells me she nearly died from pulmonary edemas in her lungs.

Sonny is instantly in love with them, and they are calling him their nephew. He wanders off with them whenever they go somewhere, leaving Mommy behind and asserting his independence. But when it is time for beddy-bye, there is no substitute for Mommy cuddles, and he's suddenly acting like a little boy again.

After a good night's sleep, we go down to the lake. I take out my kayak, they take out their paddleboards, Sonny jumps in my boat with me, and we float aimlessly in that clear, freezing mountain lake.

Tonight, we savor a full moon with no ambient light. It is one of my life's most magical moments.

We are like three kids on a camping trip. Not three middle-aged or middle-aged-plus women. We are like three giddy high schoolers leaving school in somebody's '71 Nova after second period.

A little over two weeks in, I realize the payoff of this adventure is reconnecting with people I care about but haven't seen in decades. I'm tying together a lot of loose ends. I want to know how life played out for everybody. I want to see how they changed and grew—and how they didn't. What was hard, what was easy.

Is this real? Out padding at more than 10,000 feet of elevation with Amy,
Cindiman, and Sonny

Little pieces of my life are clicking back into place with these reunions, yet I never realized the pieces were missing. They were. I thought I was nurturing these friendships online, but no.

Seeing my people here, in person, it's a whole different connection. These people went from important friends that I constantly saw when we lived close, to email or Facebook friends after I moved back to Florida. I thought electronic contact kept us connected, but now that I sit across from my long-lost friends, look them in their eyes, and feel their love, I know the difference.

It is so sweet to circle back and find out our friendships are real and alive. There is also something sobering about sharing the challenges we've battled in our years apart.

What a gift to come together and have time to sort it all out under this full moon.

SITTING ON THIS ROCK

I'm writing this while sitting on a rock at the top of Molas Pass. I cycled here on Ride the Rockies and again on the Death Ride. That second time, I summited at sunrise and had this view to myself. I drove here today, which feels like cheating.

But I am busy, just sitting on this rock. Sonny spent some time teaching me mindfulness.

A chipmunk is going to town eating the little nut he holds. I watch him for the most peaceful moment, and I enjoy learning to stop and savor things like this. I can sit here and think about people or purpose or money or health or politics, or I can watch this cool chipmunk. Or stare at a single aspen leaf flickering in the wind, or pet my dog because he is here with me, also enjoying this moment.

I do not have a single worry.

Wow, look at the shape of that rock!

Gee, listen to the sound of that little girl laughing.

Oh, and there, I count one, two, three, four, five, six, 34 dandelions in front of me.

I'm right here, right now. And because I am, I don't have a thing to fret about.

Meanwhile, Little Man is standing here, taking it all in as he always does. This trip is not a mindless romp for him. He stops to enjoy every single thing he sees, and that makes me stop, too. His wonderment makes me experience this moment ten times bigger than if I were taking it in by myself.

We are on a rocky peak at 10,912 feet, looking at a view with about 40 distant peaks, two lakes, and a million trees.

He stares to the left. He stares to the right. He finally takes a few steps and looks down at the rocks, then up at the sky, then at me. It's too steep for me to let him run off-leash, but he is free.

We go back to the van, and I give Sonny two treats. He gobbles them up, wanting more.

He savors the moments but devours his food so mindlessly. My soulmate.

INDEPENDENCE DIP

"What's going on?" "Kenny" asks as he steps into the clothing-optional hot spring where I am soaking.

"Just enjoying a beautiful day," I say. "How are you today?"

"Just hanging out." He laughs.

Yes, he says that—and he really is hanging out. Yes, I look.

I can say I'm quite sophisticated about these things, but honestly, who doesn't look?

I see Kenny look at me, too, because I am also naked/nude/in my birthday suit at Orvis Hot Springs Resort in Ridgeway, Colorado. The last time I was here, I was 31 and stopped for a soak with my friend,

Tina, while on Ride the Rockies, a weeklong, 443-mile cycling trip. Add 32 years and some poundage and, yeah, my body is not the same.

But does that mean I'm supposed to hate it? Because I don't. I love it.

My weight goes up, and it goes down, and then right back up again, but I have the most priceless thing a human being can have: a healthy body. A healthy body is a perfect body.

So, big deal. I take a nude dip in a clothing-optional hot spring. I thought about not sharing this salacious news, but what is the headline here? Middle-aged-plus woman strips down in an idyllic setting and takes a rejuvenating soak in healing waters that make her feel beautiful.

If Kenny isn't embarrassed to parade out there with body by Buddha, why should I be? Kenny's naked confidence gives me naked confidence—regardless of how low my breasts droop.

Besides, I had to go to these hot springs because the other springs open too late in the day for me to leave Sonny behind in the van. It'll get too hot. Orvis opens at nine. My friends and I used to regularly go to Colorado hot springs that were clothing-optional but sex-segregated. Orvis is the only one I've been to where there are guys in the pools, and honestly, it's much more interesting. I don't feel self-conscious. I feel terrific.

If somebody wants to have a laugh about my body, let 'em. I don't care.

So what if my body isn't perfect these days? It wasn't perfect when I was 31, either.

Kenny told me he's from Austin, recently divorced, and…

He stays with me for the next 20 minutes while a silver-haired, hot-bodied Kevin Costnerish guy bathes alone just ten feet away. I am missing an opportunity! More people filter in, and now about 20 men and women are here—half in bathing suits, half not. We all luxuriate in a lush Zen-landscaped hot spring on a perfect Fourth of July morning in the Colorado Rockies. I would share a picture, but no cameras are allowed. I'm taking pictures with my brain. I remember everything, including Kenny.

I feel at peace with my body and my life, knowing the cellulite, wrinkles, and scars aren't going to get better. Does it matter? This body lets me do so much. I'm not embarrassed. I'm not self-conscious.

I'm grateful.

ONE STEP, THEN THE NEXT

There is still plenty of sunlight, so I decided to hike up to Crater Lake in the Maroon Bells.

But I realize now I have seriously f*cked up.

I haven't hiked this trail in decades and forgot how hard and rocky it is. This is well beyond what my bad knee can handle, and the terrain tells me this might be one of my dumbest decisions in a lifetime of dumb daredevil decisions. Especially since I forgot my brace.

The Maroon Bells are an iconic set of mountains outside Aspen that are among the most photographed mountains in the country. They are in ads, on calendars, in prints, and on coffee cups.

This hike was hard for me when I was young and strong, but I forgot that. I forgot that hiking this trail means crossing rockslide fields, climbing over and around thousands of medium, large, and ginormous rocks piled on top of each other. This is exactly what my orthopedic surgeon warned me not to do.

I am at risk of falling and breaking something—or everything—because this hike is a straight-up terror, especially since I don't have my brace. It's rated moderate/challenging, but that's for coordinated people, not people like me! It's treacherous and advanced because my balance is and always was iffy, and because my knee is a mess. I have that feeling I get when I do something athletic and stupid in an area where there is no one around to rescue me.

Turn around. It isn't worth it.

That voice. It's the one that tries to talk me out of risks, and it's at it again, but I know it's right. I should turn around. It isn't worth it.

My other inner voice—the one responsible for everything fun and good that ever happens—calms me down.

One step at a time. You know how this works. You do it all the time. One step at a time. Take the next step, then the next.

There are rocks on top of rocks, yet I keep going.

Left foot. Right foot. Left. Right. Left. Right.

If I look at those massive rock fields, I'll turn around, praying I don't fall and need a helicopter rescue. But I don't look at the rock fields. I focus on the rocks, one at a time. I focus on where I put my foot. Left, right, left, right, left… I know I will get beyond this. I pass one rock field and then, minutes later, find my next set of obstacles.

An older couple stops for a drink of water on their way down, and we commiserate about our bad knees.

"Does it get less rocky?" I ask.

"It gets worse," the woman says. "You could get hurt. You should turn around and go back because it's bad up there."

I think hard about it. I have so much at stake. First, I could die—but probably not. But I could get injured and it's still early in my trip. That will ruin everything.

One of the many rock fields I encounter. Left foot, right foot. One step at a time.

There are other people on the trail, but the number dwindles rapidly because everyone but the people with Maroon Bells camping permits (like me) has to be brought in and out of the park on a shuttle. The last shuttle leaves within the hour. What if I fall after everybody leaves? That voice is doing a number on me, scaring me as much as possible.

I keep going. I want to see the lake. I want to feel like I can do this.

I don't want to be some old lady whose best hikes are all behind her. As the other hikers head down to get to the shuttle, I ask them the same thing.

"How far to the lake?"

"You have a long way," they answer.

But I think I'm almost there.

"How much farther?" I ask again and again.

"You're a little over halfway," they say.

"How much farther?" I plead.

"You're not close."

Left. Right. Left. Right.

Sonny is such a trouper. I have a hands-free leash that attaches around my waist because I use two hiking poles for stability. I sure need the poles today. After six hours of driving from Southwest Colorado and now this, I am exhausted and getting more depleted. I keep heading up.

"How far?"

"Thirty minutes," a backpacker tells me. Good God, how is that even possible? Someone told me it was a half-hour about 15 minutes ago.

I've been hiking forever.

Not even two minutes pass, and I encounter a woman from India hiking down the mountain with her family, wearing a flowing red sari, more fitting for dinner in Manhattan than this tough trail. She sails across the rocks so effortlessly.

"How much farther?" I ask, hoping for a different answer.

"Six minutes," she says. "Just six minutes. It's right beyond those trees. You are so close!"

I walk about 50 yards, and then I see it—pristine Crater Lake!

I stop for pictures with Sonny and a drink of water. He's tired, too. He wants to drink and drink and drink, but BOOM! What? Thunder.

I've been so focused on keeping my feet balanced that I didn't notice the clouds moving in.

No, no, oh God, no.

I brought no raincoat or protective gear because I thought I was doing an afternoon mountain stroll with a little bit of elevation gain. I have one protein bar. I don't savor my achievement of getting to the lake. Instead, my boy and I head down the mountain.

I unleash him on the downward trek because he could go too fast and pull me down on the rocks. Nobody's up here now, anyhow. I worry that someone with a dog will come up and we might have an issue, but nobody is coming up now. Sonny doesn't leave me. How far we have come from the days when he would run away the minute he was let off leash. He is now my little hero dog. We are so in step with each other on the descent that I feel protected. He knows I'm nervous, and he stays within two steps of me.

Twenty minutes pass, and the rumbling stops. I'm making great time on the descent, heading down way faster than I'd gone up. That's unusual on a bad knee. Down is always so much worse than up, but my two hiking poles minimize the impact, and I keep moving at a good clip.

When I make it through the rock fields, I see where I'd met the older people who told me to turn around. I know I am halfway to the bottom. And from this moment on, the trail is easier. Still a lot of rocks, but not so much rubble, and there are some stretches that are not rocky at all. I soon hear a familiar creek and know I'm getting close. Then, through the trees, I see Maroon Lake at the bottom. I am extra careful now because I know that hikers and skiers are always more likely to get hurt when they think they've licked the challenge. That's how I injured my knees in the first place—by being overconfident when I was skiing my last runs of the day.

One step at a time, I finish.

The light is golden, and I sit there on a bench, looking at the Bells for a long time and relishing that protein bar as if it were a fine delicacy. I have always loved the Bells, but now I love them even more because this hike has made me feel confident. Strong.

And young.

I can really hike now. *Really.*

Sonny is exhausted, but he stares at the Bells, taking in nature, like usual, until he sees a marmot and wants it. I rein him in.

I say a gratitude prayer. I am happy.

I'M BACK

I'm cycling up to Maroon Lake this morning when I get passed by a very fit guy who is half my age.

Imagine my surprise, just 15 minutes later, when I pass him.

"Beautiful day!" I say as I glide by.

"You're kicking my ass!" he says.

Well, yes. I am. That's not to say that my ass is not getting kicked. The altitude up to 9,462 feet is hitting me hard, and there are plenty of breathless moments, especially on the steeper grades. My heart rate is way up at 152 bpm, and it's wearing me down. I stop two times to breathe and recharge, which helps so much. Halfway up, something clicks in mentally, and I start to adapt to the thin air. I can breathe. Breathing is good.

I pass a thirtysomething couple on the way up, and they prove why tandem bikes are often called "divorce machines."

"I told you that you weren't in shape for this," says the guy, who is in the stoker position in the rear.

"What-ev-er," she says from up front.

"Just stop pedaling and make him haul you all the way up!" I say and laugh as I pass by.

She giggles.

"She's doing that anyhow!" he says.

I feel so strong! I'm getting passed, maybe there have been seven or eight riding faster than me, but I don't care. What a crisp morning in the mountains! The view of the Maroon Bells is five-star perfect, and there are virtually no cars—just the occasional shuttle bus carrying people up to the lake.

I stop for a picture in a clearing, and two women pull in behind me.

"This is a killer!" one of them says.

They are on electric bikes. Explain that to me. How is that a killer when they have motors to help them up these mountains?

I don't say a thing. When I reach the top, I take a selfie and know I can call myself a cyclist again. Never mind what I used to be able to do. I can still kick a little ass.

And I don't need a stinkin' motor.

I stay up top for only a couple of minutes, then head back, racing down that wide, traffic-free road.

I'm back.

JEANNE

Unfinished business

Sonny and I head to Leadville to see Brian and Cheryl. We have unfinished business.

Our close friend, Jeanne Elliott, died two years ago after a hard, hard life. She was shot and paralyzed in a courtroom in 1986 when she was a lawyer representing a battered woman in a divorce case. The husband in the divorce—an Aurora, Colorado police officer—came into the courtroom and shot Jeanne four times. She was only 37, and her health remained a constant battle for the next 35 years. When she died in March of 2021, all of us were shattered.

Her friend Linda wrote me a few months ago to tell me that, as she was packing to move, she came across Jeanne's hand-carved walking stick. After she was paralyzed, Jeanne passed it on to her since there would never be another mountain hike. Linda wondered if I might want it.

I thought the best thing we could do would be to return Jeanne's beautiful "MOUNTAIN WOMAN" stick back to the mountains—as a memorial. Jeanne's best friend, Tonda, agreed. We all wrote notes to wrap around the stick with yarn, and I carried it to Colorado in my van. Brian, Cheryl, and I planned to leave it on a trail at the top of Independence Pass. We made peace with the possibility that someone else might walk away with it.

But when I arrive in Leadville today and reunite with those two beloved friends, I realize the stick belongs on their mountain property where it is always quiet and no one will ever take it away.

As the sun begins to set, we plant the stick on their land, facing Mount Elbert and Mount Massive, two 14,000-foot peaks. Because we only had a virtual memorial after Jeanne died during Covid times, we can finally release our grief.

The walking stick is now there for our girl to reclaim, whenever she feels like a hike.

The next morning, Brian sees a small herd of deer around it. Just for our girl.

YOUNG

I hike every day when I am home in Florida. I swim more than a mile most days, and when I don't, I go cycling. I go kayaking one to five times a week, but that's not my exercise—it's my Zen.

I have a good life, but it has become a great rut.

It's comfortable and fun, and I am happy with it. But a rut is a rut is a rut is a rut. It's like the "Self-Transcendence 3100 Mile Race." Competitors keep running around the same block in Queens, NY, over and over and over again over 52 days. They have to do 60 miles a day between 6 a.m. and midnight. The people who do it are in incredible shape and need to be because all of those trips around the block equal 2 1/3 marathons every day around the same block!

Apparently, the repetition leads them to a place of self-transcendence, but for me, doing the same thing, day in and day out, leads me to a place of familiarity and complacency. I live a lovely life, and even though it's adventurous and filled with nature, there is a sameness to it because I'm almost always in the Tampa Bay area. If you're going to be in a rut, be in your rut in Dunedin, where I live. It's so lovely that I had trouble forcing myself to take a break from it.

Stunning view as I start cycling to Deer Creek Canyon

Stepping out of it has let me hike new trails, see new sites, visit people I've missed, and tune into life on a frequency I have never been able to process.

I wake up every morning curious about what the day will hold, since I rarely have a plan. Or if I have a plan, I almost always change it. Life is a constant surprise.

I'm doing what I want to do, setting my course and constantly changing my mind about what I want to do. It's the opposite of what the 3,100-mile race organizers describe as "self-transcendence," but it sure fills my definition of self-transcendence, which is to live above the noise in my head.

And being here in the zone of self-transcendence, I've realized something marvelous. I am getting younger every day I do this.

My day is not stuck in the minutiae of trying to be productive. I give my life to the wind, and I live it in the moment.

I got up early to cycle Deer Creek Canyon, my old Colorado training ride just outside Denver. This is a huge achievement because Deer Creek is a difficult route. It was always difficult. The last two miles are a seven percent grade, and they were a bitch even when I was 29. It's much harder on me now, but I'm getting my climbing legs back, my knee feels stronger, and I feel stronger. I am doing it!

I'm grinding up those last two miles—hating them, hating them, hating them until I conquer them and realize how much I love, love, love them. I am back.

Heading down, I keep my speed below 43 mph—way slower than I used to go. I got that life-changing concussion on my bike when I was meandering at 11 mph back home. I don't like going fast on a bike anymore. Speed used to be a point of pride, but now I think of it as a point of recklessness. I know what's at stake. One head injury is enough for this lifetime.

I finish, drive to a nearby trailhead, and take Sonny hiking because he expects his morning exercise, whether I've cycled or not.

I biked a beast and hiked a canyon. My confidence is overflowing.

I'm strong. There is no stress. I'm free. Hope is flowing.

I am young today.

DENVER, I'M NOT FEELIN' YA

Ah, Denver! My old home. The Mile High City, where the air is thin, the mountains are majestic, and the traffic is miserable. I left in 1997 and come back every couple of years. About 15 years ago, growth completely changed the vibe here. The town morphed into a fast-moving, trendy, and young city, and it feels like there is a spectacularly pretentious party going on that I am not invited to attend.

I loved it way more when the highlight of the year was the January stock show. The whole metro area smelled like cow manure. I miss the guy who used to roller skate at lunch on Capitol Hill, wearing a different colored tutu every day. What I wouldn't give to order chicken chipotle at Juanita's one more time, but Juanita's closed long ago. A food magazine ran a list of 130 beloved restaurants that have died in Denver, and when I looked at that list, it pulled so many long-forgotten moments out of my heart.

I was lucky to live here when I did. What a great place and time to come of age. But our big cow town turned itself into a major city. Denver's population has increased by 45 percent since I moved home to Florida, and the metro area's population is up by 61 percent. That brings all kinds of challenges. Homelessness has grown into a catastrophe that makes national news.

There are a lot of good reasons people think this is the best place to live in America. The brown cloud of smog has mostly cleared, the arts have exploded, sunshine is almost constant, and the Rockies still stand tall in the distance. The city's got breweries, bike lanes, culture, and sports. It's fabulous.

While Denver grew fabulous, I also changed. I went from being a spirited extrovert to an introvert who doesn't like noise or crowds.

Is this my introversion talking? Or am I just acting old? The median age in Denver is 37. The median age in Dunedin is 58. Hmmm.

I used to *love* this city, but I don't enjoy fabulous. If I were ever willing to freeze and move west again, I'd be in Salida in the Arkansas River Valley. Cool vibe, gorgeous views, and my friend Tara is right there.

But most of my Colorado friends live in Denver, so I'll be here for at least a week. I guess. As we know, there is no plan.

I drive by my old house, and it looks exactly the same. I remember my grouchy neighbor telling me, "You're crazy if you think you're going to get $165,000 for that house," when I put it on the market. I got it. I checked online, and it's since had an elegant (*fabulous!*) renovation inside and is worth almost a million dollars. They got rid of what I loved most in there—the knotty pine walls in my den, the 1970s wall-mounted oven, and the porch swing. Grrr.

Most of the roads are right where I left them, and the routes are exactly the same. But once you forget a city, you forget it. The traffic here is full-bore—as bad as the high tourist season in Florida. Nothing moves. That's Denver. Nothing moves.

I am lost here.

HOME INVASION SPECIALIST

Imagine the energy when my friend Diane and I finally sit next to each other for much-needed girl time. I haven't seen her since I moved away, and we're sharing the good, bad, and ugly of everything that's happened, when suddenly: "Ba-da-boom, ba-da-boom, ba-da-boom, ba-da-BOOM!"

A thundering beast emerges from the basement. It's Sonny Germer, who has been secretly rummaging his way through all of Diane's private space down there. He races upstairs to inspect the rest of the house.

I thought I knew my dog before we left home, but it wasn't until we started going to friends' homes that I learned Sonny's got a real passion for violating boundaries and snooping. By this point in the trip, he's made it clear that home invasion is his purpose in life.

I'm now at my friend Debby's house enjoying a similar deep conversation when I realize my dog has vanished.

"Sonny!" I call.

No response.

"Sonny!"

He emerges from her upstairs bedroom and flies down the stairs to join us.

"Ba-da-boom, ba-da-boom, ba-da-boom, ba-da-BOOM!"

An hour later, I'm at Tina's house, and he does a full-on professional investigation of every room on her main floor before heading up to scrutinize the rest of the house as if he's doing a raid on behalf of the Department of Justice.

He did this at Karin's, Michelle's, and Kyla's homes, so I think we've got a pattern here. Sure, he loves looking at high peaks, waterfalls, and wilderness, but he also loves being a crazed busybody, tearing through houses as fast as he can before he gets stopped. I have started warning people to close every door where they do not want an intruder—because an intruder is coming.

CONNECTIONS

Lunch with Joe (who saved me on the Death Ride) and his wife Rachel is soul medicine. Joe is 70, and the corporate executive look he once sported has long been replaced by a massive beard and long, white hair. The dude went hippie a long time ago.

This week is one reunion after another, and I'm finding love is still where I left it so long ago. I'm seeing everybody I can, which means stopping by people's houses, going for coffee, lunch, dinner, or just a walk.

It always starts in a superficial way. But in a few minutes, we share a familiar glance in a "we were there together before any of this" moment. Love pours into and out of my heart. We share our true stories, not the Facebook versions.

I thought hitting the road was going to be about hiking and cycling, taking pictures, and logging experiences.

It's all of that, but that's all secondary to the love.

The road has connected me to the people who mattered so much in my past. I never forgot them. I never stopped loving them. But distance froze what were close friendships into fond memories kept alive as social media contacts. If I hadn't gotten the van, I probably would have lived the rest of my life without circling back and seeing everybody, and I would never have understood what they'd meant to my life. I'm getting that now.

I can't be in all places at all times having intense friendships with hundreds of people. We use an email or a text or a like on a post to let friends know we're thinking of them. But the real way to do it is with eye contact and long hugs. It feels like home. Odd, right? Home is not just a house or a place—it's people. And so many of my people are here, so this is also my home. It's unsettling to see everybody older. In my mind, everybody stayed the same for all these years. Most stayed in their 30s to early 50s in my brain. But sitting across from each other, I see how they have aged.

While I look at them, they look at me. I'm giving them an eyeful, because I've had a lifetime in the sun, and my skin is nothing like it was when I left here at age 37. I saw a friend I hadn't seen in forever and thought, "Wow, you sure got old." I knew she was looking at me and thinking the same thing.

As I reconnect with my friends, I hear stories of health challenges that are a reminder that we must, must, *must* live right now. More than one friend has had multiple strokes. One has Parkinson's. One made it through leukemia. One is in heart failure, another has a neurological issue. One, once a super-hiker, has vertigo that won't let her drive in the mountains. One almost died with a lung issue. One friend's memory is shot, but I don't think she has a diagnosis. Every one of these men and women were athletes: They are Coloradoans. We cared about our health and did *something* physical every day, and most of us did a lot. How is that list of medical problems possible with such a group of athletes?

It is something to hear us talking about our health because we aren't lingering on the topic like some people do back in Florida. I've long said that we should all write our ailments down on index cards, then pass the cards around the table at dinner, read them silently, and nod that we have processed the info. There's no need to get caught in that loop of complaining about health issues, and these people don't do that.

But we do try to make sense of the shock of what happens as we progress through life.

One friend lost 2/3 of his pension when his company went bankrupt. His wife, who is one of my lifetime touchstones said, "Unfair things happen in life. Suck it up and get on with it." I feel that way, too. There are so many reasons to be dissatisfied, but dissatisfaction makes us unhappy. I choose to skip that step.

I should note that a couple of very lucky friends have had no medical issues. But they are definitely the exceptions.

We don't get a choice about what happens to us. All we can do is fight for our lives with how we eat, exercise, and nurture relationships, and do our best to cope—no matter what.

And when life starts to go south, we have to suck it up and get on with it.

OLD ROCKS

I sit with a friend as she frets about a certain national politician who stirs extreme feelings. He shall remain unnamed, because why go there? She is so stressed talking about him, worrying about what might happen because of him, wondering how this is happening to our country, pondering whether she can live in her own country if things get too crazy.

I pick up a rock and hand it to her.

"This rock was here long before he was," I say, "And it will be here long after."

These are scary and ugly times. They aren't resolving themselves in short order. I have to accept that these challenges may last for the rest of my life. I think that ultimately, people are good, and we will bring goodness back.

I have faith in the long perspective because, throughout history, there have been brutal, fearful times that have always ended. Civilization has survived the Romans, the Barbarians, the Dark Ages, the Nazis, famines, plagues, civil wars, slavery, and genocides. So, humanity has survived much worse than what is happening now.

People in my age group enjoyed many years of peace. I took that to mean that civilization had learned and grown from its mistakes—but I was naïve. We need to keep learning how to love one another, but as a people, we still haven't.

That has made for a lot of sleepless nights for me in recent years, and I've been trying to figure out how to live with it because it's so sad. And frightening. It's one of the reasons I checked out of my routine. I needed to see more than daily headlines of chaos and hate.

I look at the mountains and see miles of majestic wonder, canyons, desert, and snowcaps. There's a good argument that all this grandeur was created by geology, but it can't be an accident of science. I see God in all of it. That calms me because the mountains I see at this moment were here long before the bedlam and will be here long after.

For the last twenty-three days, my worries have faded as I slowed down, looked around, and found my grounding. It's a new reality.

My friend Tina and I walk Sonny in Washington Park today. I used to walk that park every day with my golden retriever, Honey, and my sheepdog mix, Buster. Honey's ashes are there. Buster's ashes were spread up in the mountains that I can see in the distance. I still love them both so much.

I miss them today, a day that is hot, hot, hot. My poor black dog, Sonny, starts to overheat. We stop under some big shade trees to let him cool off in the grass. Tina and I sit down on the grass with him and stretch out—for more than an hour. It is the most simple, calming moment—and I believe it's my favorite hour of friendship in 33 years of being close, close friends.

Stretching out on the grass with Sonny brings us the simplest peace. I never sit with Sonny under big shade trees. I have one in my own yard, but I've never sat under it once.

How much do I miss by always moving so fast rather than slowing down or outright stopping to enjoy people, my pets, or the scenery around me? I walked thousands of miles in Denver's Washington Park and never stopped like this. What would my life have been like if I had learned to occasionally sit still and do nothing? How much life have I spoiled by worrying about matters that are out of my control? How much negativity have I welcomed into my brain by letting the news of the day upset me or break my heart?

Peace was in front of me that whole time, but I never slowed down to understand it. Back home, I go to the big water (the Gulf of Mexico) all the time, but I'm always busy. I'm either walking the beach or kayaking or taking photographs or swimming. I take only one "beach day" a year when I sit in a chair and read. I should at least take two, right?

I feel more by doing less.

That becomes clearer tonight when I see my friend Ann for dinner. She is a real estate agent, a proud workaholic who *loves* her work.

I ask her what all her work will add up to when it's time to write her obituary, and she says she doesn't care about her obituary. In fact, she says, nothing would make her happier than if, on her deathbed, she is checking in to make sure her last two contracts are tip-top and ready to go. I can't relate, yet I know she can't relate to my perspective, either.

"When will your trip end?" she asks.

"I dunno," I say.

My lack of a plan is as foreign to her as her endless hard work is to me. People are different. I'm always reminding myself that different is not right or wrong. It's just different. Stop being judgmental!

A friend back home is also a real estate agent, and she keeps canceling vacations because she wants to oversee renovations on her clients' homes. Contractors delay and reschedule, and the problem always seems to be the countertops or the cabinets. She is also watching our mutual friends dying young, but she continues to prioritize everything but herself.

I'm afraid that her tombstone will say, "She always made sure the countertops were installed just so."

She finally booked a trip to Europe and came within an inch of canceling for another decorating reason, probably countertops, but I pounded on her. I invoked the name of our dear friend. "Wendy Barmore," I said. "Wendy Barmore." I said it over and over.

Wendy's shocking death said everything. Live now. Delay nothing. Wendy had released a kick-ass, raw rock album, and she was just getting started at age 67. Then she died.

Her name is a reminder not to wait for anything.

We've all been running out of time since we were born, but I didn't understand the urgency until recently. I've really started to look at my life and realize I have enough money and enough things. Happiness is not one more thing away. I have it right here, right now.

NO

A beautiful day, a restful moment of reflection, then BAM.

"Fawn, there's something I need to tell you," the text says. "I have rectal melanoma and breast cancer. Got them in 2020 and 2021, rectal first and breast second. I had surgery on both and was doing quite well. But last Tuesday, I went to Portland to see my surgeon, and the melanoma had returned. Rectal melanoma has a dismal prognosis, and that's why I didn't want to tell you. This summer, I had four visits to the University of Virginia, where I received a vaccination for melanoma. It didn't work. So, a week from Monday, I'm going to MD Anderson for a workup for an experimental trial. May have to have a serious operation on my rear end since the two previous ones were unsuccessful. I will possibly be receiving immunotherapy. Oh yes, in early August, I have an appointment to see if my breast cancer has returned. So, I would love to meet you in Banff, but I don't know if it is possible. If it is, I will be there with my ever-loving George. It's silly to say don't worry about me, but I am actually handling it quite well, so don't worry. I just hate talking about it because there is so much unknown about it. It only happens to one in ten million people. Kind of makes me feel special. Haha. Later, alligator."

Numb.

Not Jill. Not Jill.

Not. Jill. No.

I call her immediately.

"Hey, Fawnycakes!" she says, answering. "What's going on?"

"Well," I say, "Apparently quite a bit."

She laughs.

I want to gush about how much I love her and how much she means to my life, but her cheery tone is an intentional signal from her that we are not having that kind of conversation. That's the kind of talk we employ when we think we're losing our loved one. I'm guessing it's probably why she said nothing until now. She's not someone who thrives in self-pity, and she's not planning on going anywhere.

Jill had five kids and was a secretary in a small town in Kansas when somebody told her, "You have an idiot's job." She was 29 and decided she would never be in a position like that again. She went to medical school and became one of the first female forensic pathologists in the world.

I met her when I was a reporter in Denver, and she has been my confidant/mentor/chosen family member ever since. The day my divorce was finalized, I cried, "All my hopes and dreams were built around him." She said, "Then you're going to make some new hopes and dreams, and they will be even better." When I told her I was afraid to leave my friends and the mountains of Colorado for a better job in Florida, she said, "Don't let security be your dangerous anchor." She repeated that three times, and that mantra has empowered me to take risks ever since. When my mom had her stroke, Jill guided me through the uncertainty. She was the translator between the gloom of what the doctors were telling us and the potential that still existed.

The news that Jill has cancer hits me with a wallop.

She's upbeat and hopeful. "I'm going to look at this like an adventure," she says, ever the scientist. But I am crestfallen.

Most of my closest friends from my Denver years are at least a decade older than I am. I was 30 and Jill was 48 when we became friends.

Please, God. Let her beat this.

I guess those incredible friendships that mentored and grew me up came with a price I hadn't calculated: the likelihood of carrying on without them.

Jill is in her 80s. Almost all of my other best friends here are edging up to that milestone. I won't have them all with me for the duration, and I can't imagine this world without them.

Thank you, God, for letting me have them for all of these years. I've learned from them, laughed with them, and grown because of them. I have been lucky.

But in this moment, my heart is crying.

Please, God. Let her live.

MOUNTAIN KANGAROO

Little Man scans a field that has to be a few hundred acres in front of the expanse with Wyoming's rugged Wind River Range in the distance. Suddenly, he starts doing the silliest, most lovable thing as he discovers the wonders of tall grass and endless acreage.

Sonny starts wildly hopping in the air like a kangaroo. Yes, *hopping*. He is sailing five feet in the air every time, over and over and over and over again. In one 90-second video, I catch him hopping more than 50 times. I post the video, and people all over the country are cracking up at my crazy best friend.

I call him my Mountain Kangaroo.

Is he searching for something? Are there mice in the field? I ask him, but he never explains. The more he jumps, the more I realize that my boy loves, loves, *loves* wide open spaces with tall, tall grass.

Boing! Boing! Boing!

Boing! Boing! Boing! Boing! Boing! Boing!

We are in Pinedale, Wyoming, with Kathy and Tina, who joined me from Denver. I bring the video of Sonny to breakfast.

Kathy bursts out laughing when she sees the video, then Tina joins us and laughs so hard that the man at the next table asks if he can see what's so funny.

We can't stop laughing, per usual. Tina, Kathy, and I have laughed through so many vacations over more than three decades.

Kathy's 74. Tina's 76.

When Tina and I met in 1990, our friend Lisa and I were amazed at Tina's fitness. "She still does aerobics!" Lisa said, shocked that a 43-year-old could still do such a thing. Here I am with her in Wyoming, preparing to do a difficult hike in the mountains.

Tina, me, Kathy at Sacred Rim

I am grateful that Tina and Kathy are doing the hard aging first so I can learn from them.

We are in Pinedale because we want to do something away from the madness of the tourist-favorites of Yellowstone and the Grand Tetons.

Pinedale, Wyoming

They stay in a motel, and Sonny and I sleep out front in the van. They let me shower in their room. Perfect setup.

Sonny is our pack leader, and we do a "moderately challenging" hike today to Sacred Rim, which is "moderately terrifying" in a couple of areas.

Most of the hike is in the woods. To get to the top, we have to get up a steep, rocky patch, and once there, we stand next to one of those "one-false-move-and-you're-dead" cliffs. I have never understood why or how people take pictures standing on cliffs or treacherous rock outcroppings. I don't have pictures like that. I'm clumsy and—hell yes —uncomfortable up here at the top of this hike. I don't get anywhere near that edge. I walk with two hiking poles—not just because of my bad knees, but because I trip all the time, and always have.

"Wowwww," Kathy says when she sees the overlook. "We never saw this coming."

Tina at the Cowboy Bar

I take no chances up here but relish that I am standing on top of the world with two lifelong best friends.

They can still do this—and still want to. That is why they are my role models. I'm going to keep going, just like them.

NOT AGAIN

When my friend Laurie told me she was going to retire in her 50s, get an Airstream, and hit the road, I wondered if she had enough saved to stop working so young. I was also jealous.

She had a grand adventure hauling that trailer to national parks, living on the road, meeting people, and diving into life. The time came when she was ready to leave the road, get a condo and new boyfriend, and live happily ever after.

We haven't seen each other in a while, so I didn't know that she'd started feeling like something was off earlier this year. She went to many doctors until one finally told her what was going on: It was liver cancer. Ten days later, she died.

I just got the text telling me about it.

Sixty-four.

How is this even possible?

I can't believe it. Another young friend. Sixty-four?

I am aware of how unpredictable life is. I saw that with my mom and her stroke at age 66. I know I could live 30 more years or die in an accident in the next 30 minutes. But there's been so much loss this year! I'm fighting to keep my thoughts here in the light.

I am alive. Life is happening now. I will be one day closer to the end tomorrow, so I need to get on with living today.

I am in Wyoming, in the mountains, where the sky is a deep, clear blue—free of any clouds. It stretches from the peaks of these high mountains all the way to the heavens.

I feel an even louder call to hike, enjoy my friends, embrace the sky, and laugh, filling every minute with life, not loss. And when these waves of sadness come over me, I'm going to stop, look around at the mountains, take a deep breath, and feel gratitude that I am here to experience this. I *am* alive, and I am grateful.

There is no time to waste.

But still, I am so damn sad.

DON'T WAIT

I am numb because today brought more bad news.

In three days, I have learned that Jill has two types of cancer, Laurie is dead, and my friend Nancy is on a ventilator and will die any day. I came out here to find myself, but now, I am lost.

I stand on a bluff in front of the Teton Range during the golden hour and record a video for my Facebook friends.

Hi, everybody. Today I am in Grand Teton National Park in Wyoming. A lot of people have written that they would like to do what I'm doing — take off and do a big trip, see the country, and do it in a van. In the last three days, I have found that one of my dearest friends has two forms of cancer. Another friend of mine was diagnosed with liver cancer and died ten days later. And then another friend is fighting for her life. So my message today is: Don't wait. Don't wait. You never know what's coming. The one who passed away from liver cancer decided several years ago to retire early, get a trailer, and see the country. I'm so glad she did, because she died at age 64.

You don't know what's coming in your life. Don't wait. Don't wait, don't wait. Don't wait.

That is the message. It is a beautiful day today, and you only get one crack at it. Make up your mind to live your best life. Don't delay anything. Go for it. There's so much out here for you.

Don't wait. Don't wait. Don't wait.

I'm not sure how to behave. Tina and Kathy are still with me—this is their vacation, and I don't want to be a downer. But they know I'm shaken. Good people are leaving me. Every time it happens, my world changes. Even if I don't see these friends all the time, they helped make my life full.

It's going to get worse, not better. The older I get, the more I am going to have to get used to my friends dying.

But how do I get used to this? Seriously, how?

CHECKING IN

It's morning, so I FaceTime Julie, my former partner, so I can show her the view of all the Tetons. She's my anchor and a soulmate. The first thing I do every day is check in with her. We weren't the greatest couple, but we can't seem to quit each other when it comes to getting through life. We are great friends who happen to get on each other's nerves almost every day.

I shared my iPhone location with her and ten other people who said they wanted to keep track of me. Julie has turned out to be the head of the command center, not only for safety reasons but because I can't start the day without telling her what I'm seeing and learning.

I imagine us as two old ladies calling each other three to five times a day, sharing life, and still annoying each other. But that journey, like this one, makes more sense because we have each other. I love Face-Timing her and showing her what I'm looking at or something goofy Sonny is doing. My instinct is to always call Julie first.

I'm also in frequent contact with Rebecca, my partner before Julie. Most people don't understand how I can remain so close with my exes, but I love almost every person I've been involved with. Remember that I still talk to my ex-husband almost every week, and we've been divorced for 30 years! Julie and Rebecca are great friends, too.

Rebecca gets me on a cellular level. She knows how to reassure me and make me feel loved and valued, and she helps me feel centered in the insanity of this world. And my God, how she makes me laugh. She can make the most ridiculous, incisive remarks at the most inappropriate times. She's brilliant.

She has a day job, which means I can't talk to her every morning like I can talk to Julie. That'd probably drive her crazy, anyhow, because she loves her space. But if I'm upset, I call her because she knows how to make me feel better, just like that.

My brother, Jim, monitors my location, and we check in with each other all the time. He's assumed responsibility for making sure I am okay. He's all I have left of my family, so his input is important to me. Jim is the one who liberated me to get the van. Our mom was a conservative spender. She would never have bought something like this or taken off on an extended road trip. But Jim is a CPA, financial adviser, and wealth manager. When I pondered the big adventure, he said, "Do it!" So, I did it. He's been cheering me the whole time.

I also like talking to my ex-husband on this trip because he sees my Facebook posts, and I know he's a bit jealous. I make sure to rub it in a little.

"This was the trip we were supposed to take," I say. "Any regrets?"

"Yeah," he groans.

We ended our marriage but not our love.

Then there is Joyce, my bestie since I was 23. As the executive assistant in the newsroom, Joyce was the keeper of the timecards. I was a driven young reporter who always worked too much and once worked more than 80 hours in a week. I was told to report my overtime, so I went into her office and asked if I could get my timecard back so I could add hours.

"Gee, Fawn, is it even worth it?"

Those words changed my life. It didn't matter how much money I was making. Time was worth so much more. I might have needed to work a lot of overtime depending on what was going on with the news or my projects, but I always tried to get comp time, not overtime.

She became my best friend. She's had some serious health issues that have challenged her spirit. What I don't get about her issues is that Joyce was the marathon-running, vegetarian, vitamin-eating health nut. She should be the last person with health problems. We are trying to make sense of these changes that make no sense at all.

On another front, I always want cat news, and Jane, who made this adventure possible by taking care of my cats, sends pictures all the time. I call to hear what my boys are up to and check in with her. I love knowing they have adjusted so well. We don't just talk about cats. We talk about life, our parents, how we were raised, what we think of our crazy world, retirement, and the darndest things that people do. Our calls often stretch more than an hour, so she's traveled many miles with me when I'm driving. She volunteered to be a cat-sitter, but she also got stuck with me as a close friend.

The other touchstone is Michelle, who I connected with two

decades ago when she was a customer service executive for Dell and I was furious about my sucky Dell computer.

I talked about the situation when I was keynoting at a big tech conference, and Dell leaders frantically called Michelle about the bad press I was giving them in front of their vendors. Michelle stepped in, arranged to send me a new, much better computer, and so began a major lifelong friendship.

The word "sister" doesn't seem big enough for what she means to me. We do a podcast together and visit each other all the time, even though she lives in the Dallas area. I went straight to Arlington on this trip so I could hang with her. She's the one I will call in a big emergency when I need someone to take charge and deploy the troops.

Even when I'm far away, I never feel alone.

HAIR

I would love to report that I feel so free and liberated now that I am letting my hair go natural. I've had so many friends who have done that and reported that it is the best thing ever. But every time I check the mirror, I am horrified.

There has to be a better way! I need to see what it's going to look like with no chemicals on it, and if what I am seeing is any indicator, this is not going to end well. In the past year or two, I examined my white roots and thought I was 100 percent white or gray under the dye. For the longest time, I've imagined beautiful white hair and a life free of chemical hair products. It turns out, however, that I'm not 100 percent white under the color. Not even close! The top is long gray roots and a boring brown, the

Less hair than I've ever had in my life.

middle is faded mousy brown, and the bottom hair going to be no color at all because it has to go. Today is the day.

I ask my friend Carolyn in Jackson Hole if she can get me in with her stylist. She explains that there is no such thing as a walk-in appointment during the summer season in Jackson Hole. She suggests I try her husband's barber. I walk in and, for $25, the woman chops my hair shorter than I have ever worn it. I mean, *short*. This will be so easy to manage—two minutes to dry it, so that's really perfect for travel.

The cut is cute, but it still looks trashy because of the multicolored mess up top and the blech in the middle. It is soooo short. I don't look like a guy, but it is a bit butch. I have never liked short hair on me—even though my friends tell me it looks much better.

I think I look like I'm pushing 70.

I tell myself to be patient. I don't do patience.

I am so glad I have hats to cover this up.

STUFF

The first time I moved on my own, I boxed everything I had and waited nervously for the movers to come in the morning.

What would happen if I walked away from all that stuff? I wondered.

When I moved to Denver from Florida, my husband and I rented a house that had the most amazing thing—a basement! We don't have basements in Florida, and I got so excited to have a place to put my stuff. It was full in three weeks. It really was. Then I moved back to Florida and put all that basement stuff in my garage, so I never had room to park in any of my garages.

And now I have filled a five-bedroom house with stuff. I have a wonderful office, but usually work on the couch. I've gone on a few decluttering binges, but every time, the clutter comes back. I'm not a hoarder, but it feels like my stuff has control of me.

Never have I been more aware of it than since I started living in this 60-square-foot van. Everything I need is here with me.

I always remember what my friend PJ Tedrick told me a few years ago when I interviewed her for my book, *Work-Life Reset:* "I got tired years ago of supporting my stuff. I rented or owned a house to house my stuff. I paid astronomical electric bills to air condition my stuff. I paid out the patoot to insure my stuff so that, if someone stole my stuff (which happened once), I could replace my stuff. Eventually, I figured I'd get rid of the stuff and use the money to have fun. So that's what we did."

A big part of being liberated by this little van is that I don't feel so suffocated by stuff. My garage at home is packed with camping gear, kayaks and kayaking gear, dive gear, and tools. I have parked a car in my garage one time, for a hurricane. I have closets filled with my book inventory and more camping gear. I have a ton of shoes yet wear the same three pairs every time. I must have 60 dresses, 20 sweaters, 100 T-shirts, 30 pairs of shorts, 60 pairs of underwear, 20 bathing suits, 16 wine glasses, and three sets of dishes. That is not an exaggeration—and you get the point. I have too much stuff.

60 square feet of luxury living!

It feels good to pick up and go. When I'm ready to move along, I put my loose stuff in the sink and drive away.

This has made me want to get rid of my stuff at home. I used to wonder how and why people live in tiny houses, but now I admire them because I am living in a tiny van and have everything I need (except a bathroom… and a microwave).

I have a lot of life in 60 square feet.

TEX, FRAN, AND MURIEL

I was seven or eight years old when my family drove from Flint, Michigan, to see Yellowstone and the Grand Tetons in our station wagon.

We have photos of our family standing there. When we were little, Jim and I wore cowboy hats and pretended we were cowboys. I called him Tex, and he called me Fran. It was a great family moment. We had our workaholic dad to ourselves in all that beautiful nature.

When I stop at the pull-off for the view of the full wall of the Teton Range today, I FaceTime my brother and we have a moment. We reminisce about that trip, we talk about our parents, and I enjoy going there with the only person who really knew them besides me.

I've been to the Tetons several times, and they look like they always did. A long wall of shocking, jagged, snow-covered peaks so massive and long, they can't be real.

I remember Muriel, an 82-year-old woman I met on RAW—the Ride Around Wyoming—a cycling adventure in the early 1990s. We all biked up brutal Teton Pass which, at one point, has a 14.2 percent grade. There is one full mile that is consistently steeper than an 11 percent grade, which means *pain.* A seven percent grade is hard. An 11 percent grade is torture. A 14.2 percent grade is practically suicide.

Muriel climbed that pass. My friends and I stopped at the top to carbo-load on those bland old peanut butter PowerBars. Muriel got there and pulled out a pack of pink Hostess Snowballs.

She laughed and laughed with us, so happy to be strong and alive.

"I want to grow up to be just like you," I told her.

But looking at that pass in the distance, I realize I didn't. I don't laugh as hard as I did or as often. I don't power up a steep mountain and laugh. I don't reward myself with Hostess Snowballs when I think I'm supposed to be eating something flavorless and boring but with the right carb/protein ratio. I need to laugh more. I'm so quiet and peaceful, but I have to remember to be like Muriel, whose life was such a statement of wonder and youth that I still remember her so many years later.

I wish I had some Snowballs to eat in her honor. I'm sure she left this earth many years ago, but what a mark she left with me.

If only she knew.

THE FARM

After I shower at the Y, I find myself trying to force myself to enjoy Bozeman, a beloved mountain city filled with restaurants, coffee shops, galleries, and the vibe that comes with Bozeman being the No. 3

college town in America. For some reason, hanging out here is work for me, so I drive away with nowhere to go.

I find my way to a farm in Three Forks, Montana, a Harvest Host location where I can stay if I buy $30 worth of the grains produced here.

This is the best place I have ever been.

Ever.

Sonny and I are parked in the middle of 14,000 acres of farmland—about 30 minutes from Bozeman.

I am the only person camped here. I would never have planned this. Thank goodness I have no plan.

When we arrive, it is hell-hot and I wonder how we will make it all night in a van with no generator for air conditioning. I run my portable fan and turn on the engine every 30 minutes to cool the inside, but that heat won't let up. About an hour before sunset, it's still hot in the van, but the outside temperature is perfect.

Sonny and I go for a walk and experience a slow-motion sunset over thousands of acres of mustard seed. Nature Boy keeps staring at the sun, at the farmland, and at the crops, and he takes it all in instead of running or hopping through the air like the mountain kangaroo that he is. I am taking some amazing photographs, but Sonny never stops for pictures. He lives the moment like I should.

I stop to watch the sunset all the time. This one is different. With no clouds, the sky is a bright, deep orange and the sun is a blinding yellow. It looks as if I have cranked up the saturation in a photo editing app, but the colors are real, and my eyes can't believe the glory.

Bugs start annoying us, so we are back in the van, which is still unbearably hot. I leave the side door open, drop the screen, open the windows, and point the fan right at us.

We are in the middle of nowhere with the door open because it is hot as hell, and that makes me examine all the fear I let dog me before leaving home. I was certain that a psycho killer would find me on the one sliver of hidden road in the one moment I happened to be there. I now realize the absurdity of that.

I feel so safe. Guarded, really.

I sleep so hard, and when I get up to walk Sonny, he decides he wants to explore. He's right by me and I see him, but in an instant, he's gone. I look behind me, but he's not there. I see 14,000 acres of tall, thick crops, but no Sonny and no movement. I call out to him, but I get no response. I know he's panicked because he doesn't know where the road is or which direction to turn.

"Sonny! Sonny! Sonny!" The most important thing I can do is let him hear my voice, constantly, because there's no way I will ever find him, but I can help him find me. I sing the chorus of *Ho Hey!* as loud as I can: "I belong with you, you belong with me, you're my sweetheart…"

I see movement and keep singing: "I belong with you, you belong with me, you're my sweetheart…"

I don't stop, feeling so frightened because I have no idea how to find him in those crops, which are so much taller than he is.

"I belong with you, you belong with me, you're my sweetheart…"

Movement!

"Sonny! Sonny! Sonny! Come to Mommy! Come to Mommy! Sonny!"

More movement!

And then, a precious black dog emerges, so desperately happy to see his Mommy. He jumps on me, and I don't give the down order because I am so dang happy to see my dog. Finally, I push him into a sit so I can hug him and kiss, kiss, kiss his head.

He'll stay even closer from now on. I know that.

We finish our walk, and he's right next to my left knee the whole way. My watch tells me we've walked almost four miles round trip—but we never got near the edge of the property. No one is anywhere near us.

That rural quiet will stay with me forever.

I want to come back, but I won't, because nothing will ever match this.

THE LIST

I love who I am out here. I love poking along at 60 or 65 mph when everyone else is going 80 because I am in no hurry, and I love that.

Soon enough, Sonny and I will be back hiking in Hammock Park at home. I was sentimental about leaving those paths and everything familiar to me. What was I looking for "out there" with the van when I had so much at home? I asked that in my journal before I left, proof of how stuck I was.

Before I left, I made a list of what I thought I would miss. There are 21 items on that list, everything from people I love to the bathroom in my main suite to hot showers whenever I want them, my microwave, my park, my town, my big-screen TVs, my Ninja Foodi, the ice-maker in my fridge, and of course, the Gulf of Mexico.

But I only miss four things: my loved ones, my cats, home laundry, and my daily visits to the Y. That's it. I can't believe I can live without a microwave, the Gulf, or a bathroom next to my bedroom, but all of that will still be there for me. It seems unfathomable that I could fall asleep without checking YouTube or Netflix at bedtime and dozing off with it still playing, but I love the darkness of this van and how hard I sleep at night.

There isn't much in this van, but it has every single thing I need.

I'm still not sure what I was looking for when I headed out, but I am sure of what I found. It is the knowledge that I have what I need.

Not needing more is what makes me a rich woman.

THE BOYS ARE BACK IN TOWN

And now, the moment we've been waiting for…

Sonny is minutes from reuniting with his best friend—Tre Zayas—2,641 miles from home, all the way on the other side of the country in Missoula, Montana.

Patri (Tre's mom and my friend who bought her van the same day I did) and I are meeting up for a hike in Missoula. This reunion is all about getting those two black-and-white pitties together and seeing what they will do when they recognize each other so far from home.

Patri with two happy boys. Tre on left, Sonny on right

Patri is waiting outside with Tre when we pull up, and Sonny smells his pal from inside the van. His tail is wagging so hard, and he flies out the door the minute it's cracked open. He dances in a circle, wagging his tail faster than ever, smiling with his whole heart. Tre is just as excited.

Sonny's joy dance lasts 20 seconds, then he realizes his cool factor has plummeted by such a display. He struts away from Tre, nonchalant, then sniffs some grass as if he has better things to do than see the best friend he hasn't hiked with in months.

Patri and I have a good laugh, then we hike up the mountainside, joined by my friend John Frederikson.

The boys instantly go into their usual formation: Sonny on the left, Tre on the right, walking together, in step. They drink from the same water bottle, like always.

Every time they walk like this, my heart smiles. It's why I love Tre so much. He loves Sonny unconditionally. Sonny is so crazy and energetic that he has several dog ex-friends who have dumped him, usually because he steals their balls or sticks. Once he orchestrates his steal, he proudly races around them with his prize (which was really *their* prize) in his mouth. They think he's being a jerk, but I know Sonny wants them to come after him and see if they can get it, which he knows they can't because he's so fast. After this happens repeatedly, they usually dump him, and I have to have the talk with him that my mother had with me when I encountered the mean girls in junior high school.

"It's okay," I tell him. "There are people who don't like me, too. But Mommy loves you always and forever."

Tre is so laid-back that he *wants* Sonny to take his toys if it makes him happy. Tre accepts Sonny, and Sonny considers Tre his brother. A week before Tre and Patri left on their trip in May, we were walking the boys in the park and ran into Kathy, whose dog Jackson is one of Sonny's park friends. Jackson is a magnificent Doberman, and on this occasion, he started bullying Tre. Sonny is a third the size and weight of Jackson and much smaller than Tre, but he jumped right into action. He flew through the air and pushed Jackson away from Tre by shoving his back end. When Jackson wouldn't quit, Sonny blocked Jackson from Tre, growling ferociously. Kathy quickly got Jackson leashed back up, but I was so proud of Little Man. Sonny may be a wild boy, but he has a golden heart filled with love.

If he did that to protect Tre, I know he would protect me.

THE COMMUNE

"Level, trees, grass, water available, possibly electric, spacious. Short, good gravel road. Between Kalispell, Whitefish and Columbia Falls, Montana. Centrally located."

That is describing a modern Montana gold mine. It's camping space on a man named Ron's land, close to Glacier National Park and Flathead Lake. He lists his property on the "Boondockers Welcome" app. I haven't tried this yet, but here's the thing:

Camping here is free. People renting rooms in town almost always pay $300-$500. Gold mine.

"Welcome to the commune," says Jeff, a fellow camper on Ron's property. This place is stunning, with Montana's big sky and mountains in the distance. Its location is primo, which is why it's so popular. Today there are nine RV families, couples, nomads, and one individual who vacillates between kindness and verbal assault and clearly appears to be struggling with mental illness.

Jeff leaves the door to his small Airstream Basecamp trailer open, so Sonny takes that as his invitation to leap up, fly right in, and land on top of Jeff's bed. He then smells Jeff's food. He knocks a can of flavored seltzer water off the counter, and it sprays everywhere, making a mess. In spite of the invasion, Jeff still falls in love with Sonny, and Sonny falls in love with Jeff.

I love this place.

WAITING

I am in shock.

My friend Nancy is being kept alive by a ventilator and will soon die. I received this news from Jane while sitting in my hammock in a state park on Flathead Lake. Nancy's doctors don't know what caused her rapid decline, and this makes no sense. She became ill at the end of a two-week cruise where she looked like a million bucks and laughed her way through Europe with her best friend, René. Doctors say she has acute respiratory distress syndrome.

I've known Nancy has been in trouble for almost a week. I refused to believe it would come to this. I kept telling Jane that I knew Nancy, and Nancy would come back. How naïve of me. Death decides.

There is no question about her rebounding. She's brain-dead. I can only hope that, if I am in such a situation, I will have best friends like René and Jane who will be my advocates and pull the damned plug.

I can't believe we are at this point. Not again. Not another friend. Nancy is such a young 70, and soon she will be gone, like the others I've recently lost. I'm trying not to go dark, but this is too much—and it is too dark.

The message is clear. Don't wait, don't wait, DON'T WAIT. I am hearing it louder and louder inside of my head. We are all waiting for news about dear Nancy, and we can't help but take stock of what we need to do with our own lives now that we realize how uncertain our health and future are.

Life is now.

Live now because the only thing you know for sure about tomorrow is that you know nothing for sure about tomorrow. You don't know if you have many years to live or a few hours. Nancy thought she had time. So did all the others.

It's like the Kenny Chesney song, "Don't Blink."

Don't blink
Just like that you're six years old and you take a nap
    and you
Wake up and you're twenty-five and your high school
    sweetheart becomes your wife
Don't blink
You just might miss your babies growing like mine did
Turning into moms and dads next thing you know your
    better half
Of fifty years is there in bed
And you're praying God takes you instead
Trust me friend a hundred years goes faster than you
    think
So don't blink.

Nancy will die. For the rest of us, the lesson is no waiting to do what we really want to do.

I hate questions like "What would you be doing if you only had six months to live…" because they sound so trite. But really, what if? I'd be living exactly how I am living. But a lot of people don't live for now. They patiently wait to live.

I don't know when my luck is going to run out, but it *will* run out.

I woke up mad at myself because my clothes are much tighter than they were when I left, and all of this gray hair makes me look like somebody's great-grandmother.

BFD.

Why do we do this to ourselves? Pick, pick, pick at ourselves instead of celebrating how great we are *as is*?

Considering I'm not dying or dead, I think my body is pretty perfect. And all it will take is an eight dollar box of Nice'n Easy to make me look ten years younger in an instant.

I am alive and healthy.

I can do so much with this moment, and I will do it. I also am going to love who I am, as I am. I am 62, wrinkled, my roots are white, and I could lose a few pounds.

But I am here, and I am alive.

I can be mean to myself—or not.

I am going to say a prayer that God is merciful to Nancy and all who are suffering, and then I will fall asleep in my hammock, listening to children enjoying summer at a Montana mountain lake. I'm going to let the wind rock me.

I am healthy, I am alive, and I am here.

REFUSING TO GO DARK

I just got the text. Nancy is gone.

I am kicked-in-the-gut shocked, but I'm with my friend, Christine Tutty Johnson, who piled her three little kids in the car and spent hours driving to meet me at a park on Montana's staggeringly beautiful Flathead Lake—the largest freshwater lake west of the Mississippi. We are surrounded by water and mountains, and the sky is as blue as sky gets. Maybe this is the most beautiful summer day in the history of the world.

I try not to react, but I blurt, "My friend died" to Christine.

She reaches out for me, and I tell myself to pull a Scarlett O'Hara. Don't think about it now. Later. Think about it later. Calm down, calm down, calm down. Look at the water, soak in the day. Be where you are. Be present. You can think about this later, I tell myself. Don't ruin this for the kids.

Thank God those kids want my full attention.

Three-year-old Eirnin finds a flat rock, and she piles other rocks on it and tells us it is her serving tray and our picnic table is her restaurant.

"What would you like to eat?" she asks.

"Ice cream," I say.

She puts another rock on the tray and brings it to me. That rock is my ice cream. "Delicious!" I say.

Her restaurant operation goes on quite a while until her big brother breaks the serving tray rock and Christine has to go into full momma mode to settle the tear-filled restaurant drama. This is highly entertaining, even to me—someone who has always had zero patience with children. It's a medicinal distraction on this day. Joyful—almost.

Eirnin is soon "over" working as a server, so she deputizes six-year-old Annilise as the server and makes her 11-year-old brother, Eamonn, take over the rock restaurant as manager. I tell her that she hasn't any accrued vacation time and can't leave in the middle of a shift, but you know the younger generation. Nobody can tell them anything.

Annilise gave me joy in a sad moment

Thank God for that little girl, because she keeps me in that moment instead of drowning in another loss.

"What a beautiful world," I say, scanning the panorama.

"Only if you stop to take a look at it," Christine answers.

I am not overwhelmed anymore.

I feel safe, loved, and hopeful.

Later, when they head home and I am back at Ron's property in Kalispell again, it hits me. I've known Ron for two days. He loves the company of boondockers, so there are about a dozen people here today. This is a community that re-forms itself every day as people come and go, so there's a lot of conversation as people get to know each other.

Everyone is getting together to watch the movie "RV" projected on a screen tonight, but I am not in the mood. A woman asks me why I'm being antisocial. I wonder why it's any of her business.

I want to be antisocial. The Scarlett O'Hara coping strategy of denial and delay only works for so long. The time has come to think and process. I want to let Sonny be Mountain Kangaroo in the field, I want to go for a long walk, and I want to sit here watching the sky lose the light of day.

I want to understand why my friend died so young. I want to understand why the others did, too.

I tell myself, "I refuse to go dark. I refuse to be sad."

I keep telling myself that, but I spend the evening feeling dark and sad.

ROMP

"We're going to remember this moment for the rest of our lives," I tell Patri as we kayak. "But *this—THIS is that moment.*"

I slow-breathe in every second of the experience, telling myself over and over, "This. Is. That. Moment."

I can't describe the beauty of Lake McDonald in Glacier National Park. Massive mountains all around us. Fresh air. No wind. Still, still water. Bluuuuuue sky. Silence.

The boys—Sonny and Tre—are together at a pet-sitter's home near the park's entrance. Patri brought her cousin Lourdes and their friend Carol.

The photos we take are stunners, but they aren't a millionth as good as what we are seeing.

I have mostly been present and living in the moment since I left home, but I am hyper-present in Glacier.

I don't mention my run of good weather. I don't want to jinx it. But

I've had zero rain during the daytime on this whole trip. None. Nothing. Every day is perfect, and this day is the most perfect day of all.

Our kayak rentals are only for two hours, and I'm sad when we have to head in. I could linger out here, floating in the sun on this lake forever.

Patri kayaking on Lake McDonald

When we're finished, we hike a trail to McDonald Creek, a clear-to-the-bottom dream that splits off from the lake.

We aren't far from civilization, but it sure feels like we are. The only noise is the wind rustling the trees and the water lapping the edges of the creek. Divine.

"I'm going in," I announce.

Nancy's passing has conveyed a duty to live this day large and magnificent—for her—because that would be how she would want her friends to react to her passing, and for me, because that is the only way I can begin to accept it. She would have thumbs-upped what I suddenly do: drop my shorts, toss my shirt, bra, and undies to the ground, and skinny-dip there in the light of day in a busy national park in peak summer season.

"You're going in *naked?*" Patri asks.

"Goin' in!" I walk awkwardly over rocks into the water.

"Naked?" she asks again.

"Yup."

"What if another hiker or kayaker comes?"

"If they want to see my fat ass, they see my fat ass," I say.

Carol and Lourdes seem shocked, too.

"Oh, I'm not going to do that," Patri says.

"Me either," says Lourdes.

"Nope," says Carol.

Do I care? No! This is such a great moment, entering that frigid water. It is freakin' freezing, so it takes me a good while, but I go all the way in. I'm laughing so hard.

Two minutes later, here comes Patri. Naked on top, but she keeps her panties on. The other two go in like that, too, and I can't figure the point of it because they are covering up the part of the body that's concealed by the water. But no matter. This is a total delight. Four middle-age-plus women skinny-dipping in Glacier National Park. A moment for the ages.

We take the best pictures of the four of us laughing out here in this mountain creek.

This. Is. That. Moment. I keep repeating that to myself, and it's a mantra I will carry with me because we all usually get so busy taking pictures and carrying on that we forget to stop and breathe in a moment that we will remember until we die.

After 10 or 15 minutes, we climb out, then get dressed.

Wouldn't you know? The minute I zip up my shorts, a bunch of kayakers paddle past. If they'd come two minutes sooner or we'd have gotten out two minutes later, they would have seen my fufu. But not Patri's or the others'.

Not that I care. This is for you, Nancy Carney. I hope you got a good laugh.

Like the saying goes, well-behaved women rarely make history.

LATE AFTERNOON DRIVE

It's been a hugely exhausting day, what with kayaking and skinny-dipping, but I'm not wasting a minute of it. I am dictating this as I drive up Going to the Sun Road.

The biggest reason I'm in Montana is that I want to cycle up this road. I've wanted to do it since I was 30. I've trained for it and right now want to see what I'm dealing with before I start riding at 5 a.m. tomorrow. Every local who knows my plan to ride it tells me I am making a mistake.

It's not a safe road for bikes this time of year, they say.

The climb itself is exceedingly difficult, but I've trained for it. That was the point of buying a new road bike with low climbing gears, and the point of me getting up early to train so many days this summer: I wanted to come here to Glacier, cycle up this road, and achieve an unrealized goal from so many years ago. If I can get up this rough road, nobody can call me old.

I've thought about cycling up this pass every day of this trip. It's why I am camping alone in the park tonight, and why Sonny is still at the pet-sitter's house.

Montanans say this is a bad time to do this ride because of the combination of steep cliffs, blind turns, almost zero shoulder, and the endless summer traffic of tourists who are distracted by the scenery. This is one of the narrowest roads I have ever driven. With my mirrors and cargo rack on the back of my van, this is as big as any vehicle allowed on Going to the Sun Road, yet I see many much larger RVs up here. When two vehicles approach from opposite directions, there is a scary space problem. It's way worse when there is also a bicycle trying to share the road.

After the snow is plowed, Glacier opens the road for cyclists only—but for just one week. Then Going to the Sun is fair game for the mobs. The locals tell me to come back for the cyclists' week because that is the only time it's safe. But I won't be in Montana that week. I'm here now.

I want to do it so I can prove to myself that I can still cycle up anything. But after suffering such a bad head injury in a cycling accident two years ago, I'm not as confident on the road. I have lingering trauma from that experience. I mentioned earlier that the concussion was so bad that doctors thought I had early-onset Alzheimer's disease or dementia. So I'm aware that, if I have another accident and it happens on a road this steep, there is one hell of a lot at stake.

I have cycled upward of 80,000 miles in my lifetime. It wasn't until my accident that I realized how lucky I have been. My accident happened at 11 mph. When I was a Coloradoan, I used to race down mountain roads on my bike at speeds well over 50 mph, and I remember once going 55 mph. I'm so lucky I never had a wreck or a blowout at those speeds. God must have been protecting me because I never had a single close call.

This road is so narrow! But I want to do it. It has made me think about why. I realize there is a tug-of-war going on in my head between wise Fawn and wild Fawn.

Would I do this if I could tell no one that I did it? No Facebook post? No bragging rights? Is it enough for just me to know?

YES.

I want to do it for myself. I want to know that I'm still strong. I also want other people to know that I am strong and that we're not done when we leave middle age. But if I could tell no one, I would still be doing this. I know with my soul that I am doing this for *me*.

I'm driving up this pass, and this road is truly scary.
This isn't smart.
There's that naysaying voice inside of my head.
This feels wrong.

Imagine two-way traffic AND a bicycle on Going to the Sun Road

I heard that voice over and over before I left on my trip. It tries to keep me from leaving my comfort zone. Shut up!
This road is too narrow.
Shut up! People ride this road every day.
I'll be exhausted, and that means I won't be fully alert while riding.
Stop!
If I have nothing left to prove in life, why am I doing this?
I'm doing it because I've always wanted to do this! Shut the hell up!
This doesn't seem smart, and it also doesn't seem fun.
I keep arguing with that voice and…
Oh my God.

Oh my God.

Oh my God!

A man is walking on the side of the road, trying to get a picture of a waterfall, and as I pass him, a car and a motorhome come down the other side. It is so tight! I slow down as best I can, but there isn't time to stop. That man is there, and I am no more than four inches from hitting him. Four inches!

Dumb ass! Dude, you need a picture that bad?

Oh my God. My heart pounds so hard.

It hits me.

He is walking right where I will be riding in the morning. In that tiny little space on a narrow road with zero shoulder. That's where I will be. Me and my bike. With the cars and RVs.

I want to bike this road! It's been my goal and my dream!

But nearly hitting and potentially killing that man has scared the hell out of me. That naysaying voice is right.

It isn't trying to talk me out of something hard. It's trying to talk me out of something dangerous. Riding this road is *not* smart. It feels wrong. It's too narrow.

I've already had a cycling accident that wiped out my ability to think right for well over a year. I couldn't do any work for months. When I was going through that, I worried I would never get my life back.

I have my life back.

Why am I willing to risk it again? I am not invincible.

And another thing: All of the Going to the Sun Road YouTube videos make it look like a mystical, magical ride. Driving it, it's gorgeous. But it's no more stunning than Independence Pass outside of Aspen or Trail Ridge Road in Rocky Mountain National Park. It's certainly no Mount Evans near Idaho Springs, Colorado. YouTube put some sort of magical crown on this road, and it's a truly majestic pass. Gorgeous. But it's just a pass. I don't have to do this. I've done all those other rides, and they were more difficult.

That's that. This road is unsafe for me. I'm not going to do it.

I have blown up my one big goal of the trip.

But I am ever learning. I'm finding a way to balance the wild Fawn with the wise Fawn.

SOLO HIKE

Instead of cycling, my Plan B is to hike up to Avalanche Lake today. Sonny is still at the pet-sitter's house, and something is definitely missing as I hike without my main man.

The path to Avalanche Lake is a high-traffic trail, but that's fine by me because the activity means no grizzly bears. And one thing about adventuring in Montana: There is constant talk about grizzlies, bear spray, and risk. I get that.

But here's something I don't understand. Everybody hikes at least an hour to get to Avalanche Lake. The trail leads us to a little beach where almost every hiker stays jammed together on the little strand of beach where the trail ends. But a few steps away, there's another trail going around the lake. It's not hidden. Everybody can easily see it. If all those hikers would just walk three more minutes, they could have what I have: a silent, private view.

I am by myself, sitting next to a treasured national park lake and looking at a massive, cascading waterfall. But I'm also looking at those knuckleheads who did the same hike I did but stopped at the first access to the lake. They position themselves in pictures so they can cut everybody else out and make it look like they're the only ones there, which they are not. They will post photos that make it look like they hiked to a desolate, secret place and found their own bit of serenity all by themselves.

I think people do that with their lives too. They put in just enough effort to achieve the minimum, but they don't push to go further. For me, the magic in life has always come when I take the extra steps.

I sure do miss Sonny. He would have loved this, and I would have loved it more, watching him process the grand peaks, the waterfall, and the lake.

I've been here for quite a while, and a woman named Kathy just walked up and joined me.

"I feel so rich," I say.

"I know exactly what you mean," she answers.

Wealth has so little to do with money. "Have you ever noticed that really 'rich' people never seem to be satisfied?" Kathy asks. "Material things are never enough. They always want more."

"What I have is always enough," I say.

"And that is why you are rich."

True, true, true. There is nothing as priceless as what I was looking at, and I didn't pay for it. I earned it with my hike.

We don't exchange info, but I do feel like I just met a kindred spirit.

It was a delicious day. Back in the "real world," so many of the people I adore in life are fretting. Work, work, work, task lists, challenges, opportunities, collaboration, blah, blah, blah. It's all those matters that some people think will lead them to fulfillment. Some are called to it, some are trying to do what other people expect or respect, but they are constantly trying to impress and advance. Many, many people *do* feel fulfilled by all that jazz. Just not me.

I'm too busy looking at the stream I'm sitting next to, thinking how clear the water is. Or how good the trees smell. Or how grateful I am that I am alive today. I realize this sounds like 1960 flower child ramblings, but what I know is that I'm the happiest I've ever been, I sleep better than I've ever slept, I am more in my skin than I have ever been. I feel like I'm exactly who I am meant to be.

I have always tried to be as authentic as possible, but there is a peace inside of me as I sit in my dirty clothes on a rock in the mountains. It feels good not to strive for anything other than the next step on the trail. It feels good to sit and think about nothing.

Or listen to nature, because if I stop to do that, it will speak to me.

TROUBLE AT THE COMMUNE

Sonny and I are back to Ron's property in Kalispell after camping in Glacier and Whitefish. Eight people are hanging around, talking in a circle. Sonny and I joined them.

I don't notice when Ron's cat comes into the circle, but Sonny lunges at it. Sonny lives with two cats and never chases cats outside, so

I'm not sure what's up, but I yank him back, and he immediately stops. I apologize, and Ron says, "That was nothing."

But then...

"How dare you bring a pit bull here!" screams a lady in a long trailer. "Get by your van!"

My mouth is agape, and since most of the people in the circle weren't here when I camped a few days ago, I feel vulnerable because I am the outsider.

She summons her husband and two kids into their trailer then slams the door. Slams it!

What?

I am sensitive about people maligning pit bulls, and I've got to talk about this. Ever since I took in Vinny, a starving and injured brindle pit bull Chow mix that walked up to me on a busy road in Tampa, I've been hooked on this breed. I used to rescue golden retrievers and had a sheepdog mix. But after Vinny stole my heart, I've been a pit bull rescuer. I have had four great ones over the past twenty years.

Pit bulls do *not* have locking jaws. They are not naturally aggressive dogs and, in fact, pass the temperament test with better results than dozens of breeds, including golden retrievers, bulldogs, Chihuahuas, dalmatians, English setters, schnauzers, greyhounds, sheepdogs, Australian shepherds, most poodle breeds—do I have to list all the breeds? I am super sensitive about the judgment these dogs get. Most good pitties get lumped in with the bad ones, and that is why they have a 93 percent euthanasia rate in shelters. This country is killing more than a million pit bulls every year.

Most pit bulls are priceless and precious. Sonny Germer is absolutely priceless and precious.

On this day, a dog lunged at a cat.

That is the headline.

Yes, Sonny did lunge at Ron's cat. He stopped as soon as I pulled back on him. Nobody would have said a word if the lunger had been Reggie, my beloved last golden retriever who was much more aggressive than Sonny. If it had been Reggie, people would have laughed at the never-ending war between cats and dogs—ha-ha-ha. But when a pit bull does it, it's a national crisis.

"Look at what you've done!" says the one woman I know here—the one Ron said he would like to see move on. "You broke the vibe!"

Ron tells me, "You are welcome here. You can stay as long as you'd like."

But I want to leave. The minute the sun comes up, I am outa here.

WHEN IT FINALLY RAINS

I am sitting in front of the big field on Ron's property, watching the clouds forming overhead as I write Nancy's obituary.

"...Ms. Carney died on Mick Jagger's eightieth birthday, something that would have given her satisfaction, especially since she'd spent a fortune on tickets to see The Rolling Stones—her band. During her life, the 5'11" Ms. Carney evolved from beauty school dropout into a natural salesperson, Club Med employee, savvy businesswoman, and always reliable, tree-hugging liberal."

Art collector. Cat lady. Former smoker with COPD. Beloved friend.

I put it all in there and wonder if it's enough. She was so much more than my words can describe.

But I condense this friend's 70 years into one little article, and it makes me so sad. Heavy raindrops start falling from the clouds for just a moment, and then the rain stops. It's the only rain I have had since I left home, and it comes right on time.

CHILL

Jen Shryock and I met nine years ago in Missoula, Montana after I gave a speech, and we became instant friends. At the time, she was in a wheelchair, exhausted, and beaten down by rheumatoid arthritis and other serious autoimmune disasters.

Since then, she radicalized her diet, which changed so much. She has moments of blissful good health. But also, the opposite. Her life swings between strength and incapacitation.

Before she became sick, she'd been a fearless athlete and outdoors-woman—an extraordinary hiker, climber, snowboarder, and the absolute definition of a mountain badass.

Now there is no predictability or schedule for the good days or bad days. She can't will herself well, but she does will herself to do well with whatever life gives her. She's a positive person, but truthful. She doesn't cover up what is happening, but she is always pushing toward strength and better days.

When I first got to Montana, she was too ill to get together for a visit. But before I left the state, POW! She rebounded and wanted to see me. She made the long drive up from Great Falls to the Kalispell area, right before I moved on to Canada.

I am overjoyed to see her.

We have dinner, then breakfast at her aunt's, and then this morning, we go kayaking.

I can't imagine a life that moves so constantly between debility and strength, but today she definitely out-kayaks me.

Eventually, she tires and reclines in her kayak. We both float here on the lake, enjoying the sun, the mountains, and our friendship. It's like being a kid on summer break, stretched out in kayaks in the middle of Whitefish Lake on a warm July day.

Ageless and blessed. I will keep this moment with me forever.

Jen Shyrock teaching me about life

SCORE!

I'm not sure where I'll spend the night, and I start pondering options with Jen. I need to be in Banff, Alberta tomorrow afternoon to catch up with Patri, so Jen strongly encourages me to go to East Glacier to enjoy the remote Many Glacier region of the park before I go to Canada. It's out of the way, I'm tired, and I don't see how it can be any better than what I'm already looking at, but she swears East Glacier is even better.

The campground there has no sites available, but Jen *knows* Glacier. She tells me to park my van stealth at the lodge and sleep in the parking lot. No one will notice me because the parking lot is across a street and elevated above the main grounds.

Well, why not?

Jen is right. Many Glacier is a total win.

I fall in love with it because its isolation means there aren't many people here. It takes real effort to get here, but the payoff is these panoramas. They are massive and right here SO BIG.

I sit in a rocking chair on the back deck of the lodge, Sonny at my side, watching the best sunset we've seen in Montana. Once it's down, we walk out front, climb up to the parking lot, and get in the van. I put the privacy shades up over the windows, and Sonny and I crash for the night.

Rooms at the historic Many Glacier Hotel cost upward of $700, but space in this parking lot is free. I enjoy the same view as everybody else.

Free of charge!

Unfortunately, somebody blows our solitude when they shut a car door near us at about 11 p.m. and Sonny launches into full-on protection mode.

He explodes into deep woofs and growls, starting at full volume and then reaching a pitch louder than I'd ever heard. Sonny will protect his little home and his mommy in the van.

I am always reluctant to quiet Sonny's barks when he's trying to protect me because I want that protection. Most of the time. But this time, I have no place to relocate to if we get the boot.

"Shhhhh," I say, pushing him down onto the bed. "Shhhh." I kiss his head. He keeps trying to get back up, but I hold him down as he growls in the direction of the intruder's car for a few more minutes, but he doesn't bark again.

I immediately fall asleep.

I can't believe I'm living like this. I know some of my executive friends will judge it, but whatever. I love it. I am free and seeing our country.

HI, BEAR

"Hi, bear!" I shout. "Hi, bear!"

Grizzlies are an issue in Many Glacier, and Jen told me what she does to keep them away. You want the bears to know you're there. They don't like surprises. So, keep making noise. When Jen hikes, she yells, "Hi, bear!" over and over, and since I had no desire for my own bear story, I shout "Hi, bear" about eight million times.

I only have time for a seven-mile trail this morning because I'm meeting Patri in Banff this afternoon and have to drive 260 miles to get there. Sonny and I are out early, which means we are practically alone. That's great for someone who relishes alone time in the wilderness, but not great because of the bear thing.

I see bear poop—several times. My can of bear spray is in my pocket, and I'm ready to grab it. I have no idea how good my reaction skills are in an emergency, especially since my first instinct is probably to protect Sonny. And if Sonny sees a bear? That will *not* be good. He'll go straight at it, trying to protect me. If a bear sees Sonny? That idea scares me the most.

I want every bear to stay as far away as possible.

"Hi, bear!"

Nine days ago, a woman was mauled to death midday by a grizzly in Yellowstone, right as I drove through that end of the park.

"Hi, bear!"

Sonny and I trek past Lake Josephine and over to the sublime Grinnell Lake. Once we take the split to get to Grinnell Lake, we see only a few people. When we get to the lake, it's just the two of us. Grinnell Falls cascades 960 feet down the mountain in front of us.

I love nature, but watching Sonny take it in is what I love most on a hike. His eyes are wide and observant, and he looks lost in his thoughts until he catches a new scent. What on earth is he thinking? He seems to appreciate it on such a human level. Maybe he was once Sir Edmund Hillary, Meriwether Lewis, or John Muir. Or maybe even Grandma Gatewood.

He stretches out in the dirt, ready for a good nap. Sadly, there's no time to dawdle. We have to get driving.

More bear poop on the trail, but no bears.

Another hiker told me she saw a moose in the creek next to the trail —about a quarter of a mile away—so I'm excited. She says she marked the spot with some rocks.

I wonder what I'll do when I see it. Shout "Hi, moose!" maybe?

I find the rocks, but no moose.

We finish our hike, hit the road, and cross into Canada.

My God. I drove all the way from Dunedin, Florida to Alberta, Canada.

JUST TELL ME Y

I pull off for lunch. Sonny hops on the couch to sit next to me, then he sticks his nose in my armpit and sniffs. So, so rude.

But he's right. Mommy stinks.

My last shower was two days ago. Two days! I've kayaked and hiked and slept in the van and done heavy road time. I am more than a little ripe. I can pay for showers at community centers or truck stops, but my YMCA membership has been my ticket to glorious hot showers when I'm in a city. The staff treats me like family, and I love checking out the different facilities because I'm such a believer in the Y.

The one problem going there for showers is that I have to leave Sonny in the van. I won't leave him in a hot van, so I leave the van's engine running so he has the air conditioning blasting. This is a challenge because my van won't let me lock the doors from the outside if a key is in the ignition. When I shower, I use a steering wheel lock and hope I'm faster than a professional car thief.

Usually, I don't worry too much because I get in and out fast.

But now, Calgary.

Calgary has seven YMCAs, and I have somehow found my way to the Brookfield Y in Seton. This is the biggest YMCA *in the world*. I drive up to the biggest YMCA by accident.

It takes me so long to get approved for entry that I am in full panic about Sonny being alone in the van. I finally get to the locker room—which is so large it could have handled 300 people—and I take a superfast shower, then race back to my van. Unfortunately, this Y complex is so big that I get confused and exit through the wrong door.

My van isn't in the parking lot. It is *gone.* I am on the verge of tears, frantic that something has happened to Sonny who has been waiting in the unlocked van, unattended, with the engine running. Someone may have stolen the van, but I'm panicking about Sonny. Where is he?

I scan the lot and realize I'm not even in the right parking lot. This Y is that big—as big as a shopping center.

I go back in, retracing my steps to the giant pool slide that I saw when I first entered the building, then exit there. Instant relief. There is the van!

When I slide the side door open, Sonny wakes up, wags his tail enthusiastically, and covers me with kisses. I lose it and start crying. I realize I'm exceedingly tired because that was a serious, irrational overreaction.

But Sonny has been at my side 24/7 for four years, with me through the Covid years, changes in my career, many thousands of miles of hikes and walks in the woods, up mountains, on beaches, and all over town. We've done so many sunrise and sunset paddles and numerous vacations, and now we have traveled thousands of miles on this trip. He protects me, and I protect him. I love him more than I ever knew I was capable of loving anyone. My job is to protect him and give him the best day of his life, every day.

I can't lose him. I feel like I put him at risk, although realistically, what thief would break into a van with a barking, growling black-and-white pit bull protecting his home? Even though I know that Sonny and most pitties are total sweethearts, intruders will likely turn and run.

We head to Banff, which is the first place I smell and see wildfire smoke. It isn't overwhelming and, if I look in a different direction, the air is clear. So it's not a big deal.

What is a big deal is that it feels like there are more tourists here than in any place I have been, anywhere. More than in Hong Kong or China or India. It feels like there are millions of people in town, jammed together and pushing down the sidewalks like a mob. Is this a sign of what's to come? I know the West Canadian Rockies and Icefields Parkway have a lot of tourists, but I have never seen anything like this. The town population increases 500 percent every summer. There's no room for this kind of foot traffic in a small town like this.

But Banff is the gateway to the most stunning scenery I have ever encountered, so if a crowded town is the cost of seeing Alberta, I am making peace with it.

I catch up with Patri and Sonny's BFF Tre. The boys give each other their classic waddup head lift and immediately get back into BFF formation.

After eating Indian food, we go to the Johnston Canyon Campground, one of Canada's national park campgrounds. Unlike US national parks, the Canadians provide hot showers.

Two showers in one day. I am starting to feel human.

AND THAT'S WHY I'M HERE

When Sonny and I hike Johnston Canyon, it feels like we have joined an endless conga line of hiking tourists. The foot traffic to the falls is so busy and tight that it spoils the experience.

I stop for three minutes to count the passersby. Three minutes—137 hikers. That is *absurd*.

I came to Canada to get away from it all, quietly soak in the glory of nature, and chill the f*ck out. The scenery is everything I love most in nature, but "more." More rushing water, more striking canyon walls, more vivid color in the sky, rocks, and water. It's unbelievable, yet it's ruined by these crowds of noisy tourist invaders.

Like everyone here, I take pictures that make it look like Sonny and I are exploring this wonder by ourselves. The photos are lies. I should take a picture showing the masses around me, but I want to forget them.

Back at camp, I am in a bad mood. I can journal about what's eating me, but why? It was the only negativity I've felt since the day I left. It hits me hard because I'm out of practice with my grumpy side.

The good thing is that this is instantly resolved when I climb on my bike during the golden hour before sundown and ride for a little over an hour on the Bow Valley Parkway in Alberta.

I am out here, looking at the same mountains that first grabbed my heart three decades ago on a trip here with Geoff. I had rented a bike in Lake Louise and biked alone to Banff, where we were staying. I'm riding at the same time of day as that 1991 ride and reliving one of my life's most vivid, pleasant, impactful moments. That first ride here was when I fell in love with cycling. Before sunset, the sun turns the grass golden, the sky its deepest blue, the pine trees their deepest green. The mountains glow gold, yellow, white, gray.

And now, I ride past Castle Mountain, where the peaks of the 9,075-foot wall of stone make this the biggest castle anywhere. I remembered the light hitting the mountain the exact same way more than 30 years ago, and that makes me feel sentimental and grateful. It also gives me something I wasn't expecting: one of the best bike rides of my life. I'm not going far, I'm not pushing hard, I'm setting no records. It isn't difficult or easy. It is simply the best bike ride of my trip.

I'm happy.

Doug and Teri fly in tomorrow. They have been two of my best friends for the past 20 years, and we have traveled many, many miles together. It feels like home is coming to me.

DOUGIE. TERI. OH, HAPPY DAY

Years ago, I did a kayak expedition led by an incompetent guide who got me and five other paddlers lost in the Ten Thousand Islands area of the Everglades. That's the part of the Glades located in the Gulf of Mexico, not the swamp. The guide launched us in foggy weather with dangerous currents. Visibility was horrible all day, and we spent much of the time feeling lost at sea because he hadn't brought a GPS—just a compass—and all we saw was water all around us. We feared we would spend the night drifting farther out into the dark nothingness of the Gulf, and all of us later admitted we contemplated dying out there. In the last moment of daylight, we saw an island where we could land and camp. We'd been paddling for more than 12 hours in horrible weather. After I set up my tent, I got my flip phone out of my dry bag and saw I had one bar of cellular service.

I didn't call 911 or the ranger station. I called Doug.

As long as Doug knew I was missing, I would be found. "Don't worry," he reassured me. "You're on land, and you have food. You are safe there." I just needed him to know I was out there, lost. I wanted to wait for the morning to see conditions before calling the National Park Rangers. Day broke, and my fellow paddlers and I were astounded to see what the fog had been hiding the previous day: There were islands everywhere. The previous day, our inept guide couldn't find any of them with that compass. We thought we were lost in the wide-open sea.

It was a beautiful day. I was safe, and Doug didn't need to drive down to the Glades with his boat to find me. But I knew he would have.

Doug has been that guy in my life: the one I count on when I don't know what to do. He acts gruff and insensitive, but he has my back.

I am as close to his wife, Teri, and she's the opposite of Doug—understated, quiet, and a great listener. She's seen me through losing my parents and two long, important relationships. She hears me and gives unconditional support. And she is so funny making deadpan remarks about the silly things Dougie does.

He's the one who would have rescued me in the kayak adventure, but she's the one who would have given me the therapy afterward.

They take a shuttle into Banff from Calgary, and Sonny and I meet them in their motel room.

"Hey, kid," Doug says when I see him. If I cry, he'll get all gruff and say, "Aww, come on," but I'm really holding it back. Sonny does not contain his joy. He jumps, squirms, does his happy dance, and then leaps on their bed. He can't stop kissing, kissing, kissing Uncle Dougie and Aunt Teri because he is certain they have flown all the way to Canada from Clearwater, Florida—just to see him.

We've been laughing together for two decades and have traveled as couples when I was paired up, and we are thankfully still at it now that I am solo. Yes, I'm a third wheel, but I have never once felt that way. Besides, Sonny evens it all out.

It feels like I've been holding my breath for a very long time and just exhaled.

LET'S WEAR OURSELVES OUT

Teri sits up front with me and Sonny and his Uncle Dougie take the back of the van. Sonny wears his biggest clown smile because he is delighted to have man-time with his uncle. He loves guys, and Dougie is his No.1 guy. As we explore the Icefields Parkway, the men are in the back hanging out and probably talking about football.

First, we hike up Tunnel Mountain, a nice trail near town that gives us a nice view of Banff. Then we venture to Lake Minnewanka for lunch.

I don't need to recite the travelogue because we don't stop moving at all and the day has been thoroughly taxing. I feel like collapsing into a coma in the van, but Doug wants to do more and starts pushing me to kayak with them while they canoe at sunset on the Bow River in Banff. I am too tired.

"You guys go," I say.

"Awww come on," Doug pushes.

"No, I'm worn out."

"Come on!"

Finally, I come up with a solution: I'll get in the canoe with them. That way I won't have to further exhaust myself by assembling, disassembling, and cleaning my origami kayak after everything we've done all day. I can just get in the canoe and have a leisurely paddle.

I have zero energy and haven't been in a canoe in 25 years, so why not take the back seat and steer? My mistake. I zig-zag like a big ol' dum-dum for the first 10 minutes but finally figure out how to steer, and we head into the most idyllic sunset I've ever paddled. It's cold, but dammit! Who *wouldn't* want an adventure like this, cold or not? Here I am with two of my best friends, heading straight into the wilds of the West Canadian Rockies—in a canoe.

I am going to sleep SO hard tonight.

I NEED A BREAK

We hike early and avoid the conga line. It is a what-I'd-dreamed-of experience, so now I know that the trick is to be first on the trail.

Later, I record a podcast at the Fairmont Banff Springs Hotel and have a glass of wine on the hotel terrace with Teri. It feels like such a civilized, sophisticated thing to be doing after hanging out in a van for months.

When I get back to the van, I crash. I mean, *crash*. I am exhausted. I take a Covid test, wondering if that's why I'm so drained, but the test is negative. I'm so tired. I have done too much for too long, and the wear and tear of traveling like this is catching up to me.

How much longer can I keep up this pace? I've got to rally. My friends flew all the way out here to be with me. But I just want to sleep for a very long time. FYI, I saw this headline today: "Two Injured After Car Goes Off Edge of Narrow Going to the Sun Road." So glad I chose not to cycle that road.

The car plummeted 200 feet down the side of the road. The driver was thrown from the car, and the passenger was trapped inside. Rangers had to rappel to rescue them.

Ugh. I think about that as I doze off.

NORTHERN LIGHTS

We're driving the Icefields Parkway today from Banff up to Jasper. It's one of the most celebrated, scenic roads in the world. We stop so many times, and every time I take a picture, I think how great the photo is and how sad it is that the picture is not nearly as mind-blowing as what I'm looking at. The pictures are unreal. The real thing is indelible.

Our waiter at dinner pulls out his iPhone and shows us a video he shot the night before when the Northern Lights made an appearance in Jasper.

I have always said my life has been too filled with adventure to ever have a bucket list, but...

Africa, Southeast Asia—and the Northern Lights.

Northern Lights! Here? Here! Northern Lights were right here yesterday!

We immediately book a trip with the Jasper Planetarium. They'll pick us up in a van and take us to the best possible spot to see them. They have a different astronomy program in case the lights don't appear.

All of us are giddy at the prospect. Northern Lights!

As the day wore on, the app that charts the likelihood of seeing the lights shows that the odds aren't great, but they aren't horrible. We load into the van at 10:30 p.m. and are driven to a very dark field where the planetarium had specialty telescopes set up for stargazing.

Here's a star, here's a planet, there's Mars, there's Jupiter, there's Saturn.

Yeah, so? We want the Northern lights. Nothing. No light show, not tonight. Bust.

Waaahhh.

I want to come back with a story that says, "I saw the Northern Lights when I was in Canada! That was the biggest surprise and the best thing on the whole trip!"

But instead, I have a story that goes like this: I paid $65, went to a field in the pitch black of night, and saw a bunch of stars and planets with two of my best friends.

Or maybe this story: I didn't see the Northern Lights—only darkness and stars. Every time I see a night sky like that, I realize how small my problems are. I thought about that with God.

NASA says there are 200 billion, trillion stars in the universe—ten stars for every grain of sand on Earth. There are two trillion planets.

And here we are, under all of that. I feel so small and so large at the same time.

Am I just one little person under 200 billion, trillion stars, or am I one with all of them? Sounds a little woo-woo, but it makes sense out here.

There is a sacred silence in stargazing, and I've experienced it in the desert, in Hawaii, in the Dry Tortugas, and on remote beaches. I can see stars every night from my driveway, but not many. If I make an effort to get away from ambient light, I can see more.

When it's just me and a friend or two under an infinity of twinkling stars, I get a lot of perspective. We are so small. Our problems—the ones we fixate on—are minuscule. We are here for such a short time, and we get so wrapped up in our own selves that we think we are the center of the universe. The universe has no center.

I look at the stars and remember that. I am not the center of the universe.

There are more than 8 billion people on this earth. My problems are not the worst of all 8 billion people. Or the worst of the 336 million people in the US. Or the 25 million who live in Florida, or the 36,000 people in my city. If I stop fixating on myself, I realize my problems probably aren't even the worst problems in the group of ten people out here looking at the stars right now.

I say a prayer in gratitude for the beauty and the friendship I am blessed with. What a beautiful moment.

No Northern Lights. But I can't complain about sitting under a billion, trillion stars.

1 A.M.

I just got back to the van. Sonny and I are camping in a public parking lot in Jasper, and it feels especially luxurious because Doug and Teri spent $400 for a bland, way-too-small motel room. I just had to pay $15 to park here for the night with a bunch of other RVs. I have my own warm bed, propane heat, and the protective dog who has made it possible for me to travel feeling the same amount of love and security I had in the past when I was married to or attached to someone else. Different, of course. But I never feel lonely, and I always feel safe.

I have hiked and biked and kayaked, but if I'm being honest, I've done a terrible job with self-care on this trip because I haven't eaten properly or hydrated well. I haven't put any effort into cooking in the van, so without a microwave, I'm eating a lot of garbage. It's hard travel when a shower is not at the ready, when I don't have full electricity, when I'm not in an area with good stores or lots of ice. I'm exhausted. I can tell I've put on some weight because my clothes aren't fitting well. I'd be pissed about it, but good grief. I'm having so much fun! And I'm healthy.

I feel the need to be home for a while.

There, I said it.

But I know that if I go back even a week early, I will be mad at myself. I will get back, clean up, rest up, feel good, and then, after I get a few good nights' sleep, I will want to be in this van doing what I'm doing now.

I still have no idea what route I'm taking back home, and I start heading back that way in three days. I don't know if I'm taking a northern, central, or southern route. Isn't that crazy? I haven't told friends I'll be in their area when heading back because I have no idea what area I'll be in.

I left home with no plan, and it occurs to me that I still have no plan.

Why am I still up? I just said I am exhausted.

Too exhausted to go to sleep.

TMS

I need a time-out to do laundry and be a little reclusive in the van. We just got back after driving back down the Icefields Parkway from Jasper to Lake Louise.

I'm sitting here in this jam-packed van, and I think I should take some notes about it. There was a term in the news business, "TMS," for when you had "too much shit" in your lead paragraph or headline. Well, this van is total TMS.

I have been traveling with everything I *might* need and have an inability to access most of what I brought because everything is stored on top of or below something else. My packing SUCKED. I was warned to pack light by every long-term RVer I know, and I thought I wasn't bringing much. Delusional.

Next time, much is going to change because I have discovered that they have these wonderful things located all over the US and Canada called "stores."

Here is where I messed up:

- I brought enough clothing to go three weeks without doing laundry. That meant I had a pile of dirty laundry and no place for it. I shipped a bunch of clothes home ($80 at the UPS Store!) and did the wash once a week. Next time, I'll bring one week's worth of clothes and two weeks of underwear. That is it.
- I need two sets of makeup. I just do.
- Why did I bring a big cook set? I don't cook. One small saucepan is plenty.
- I worried so much about what I would do without TV or Netflix, so I bought an Android tablet that would let me stream everything. I have used it twice.
- I brought so many books. I need only one, in case I want to read anything, which I probably won't because I'd rather write. But if I need another one, I can easily get one because people leave old books everywhere.

- I did not need a month's worth of canned goods. Again, stores.
- What I needed was six months' worth of lotion because I've been so dry in this part of the world.
- What was I thinking bringing that pressure cooker and smoothie maker? I rarely have electricity to power them, and they take up a ton of space. Plus, I'm not cooking.
- Leave the car wash tool, shade tent, wine, wine glasses, plastic dresser from Walmart, half of the prescriptions, and most of the first aid stuff. Also, leave the Mexican Train game set. I never touched it.
- I have not used my GoPro and barely touched the rest of my camera gear. The iPhone did fine.
- The best thing I brought was a USB rechargeable fan. I will get another one.
- Maps are critical for when the GPS goes out.

A SPOT OF TEA

I have never wanted to get up early for sunrise, but I have never regretted it. I didn't want to get out of bed today, but the payoff will stay with me forever.

Today, we are on the trail at 7 a.m. to hike to the mountain tea house at Lake Agnes. The hike starts at Lake Louise, which is the No. 1 tourist attraction in Alberta. There are so many people in the area, and anyone who can handle the 4.5-mile steep hike up to the tea house does it. I made sure we were at the front of the conga line.

Some might describe the hike as ethereal, but it is kicking our asses.

We are some of the first to arrive at Mirror Lake along the way. With zero wind, the water is a mirror, as advertised.

Sonny stops for a long look, then a man yells at me because I've let him off leash for a photo opp. I know better. I am wrong, but that shot of Sonny staring at the reflection in the lake captures a moment I will treasure.

By the time we reach the tea house on Lake Agnes, faster hikers have scored all the tables, so we wait about 30 minutes and then have a table. Later, hikers will wait hours to sit at this mountain tea house where everything has to be carried up by the staffers hiking up to work.

Sonny at Mirror Lake

The air is so cold! I savor my tea because it warms me. This tea house is magical, but an hour later, it's chaos. The mob has arrived.

The tea house at Lake Agnes

Too much, too much, too much.

We hike down to Lake Louise, and I stop to breathe it in again. That turquoise water with the glacial mountain backdrop—I *have* to kayak that lake. Immediately. When will I be back? Thankfully, Doug and Teri encourage me and don't mind waiting.

We put Sonny in the van so he can nap, and I carry my Oru kayak to the water and launch it.

Paddling Lake Louise

Canoe rentals cost $120 US an hour at Lake Louise, and tourists wait in a two-hour line for one reason: to take a canoe out and snap a picture of them canoeing in the lake in front of those mountains. All I have to do is assemble and launch my origami kayak, and I am on my way, for free. This kayak was a great investment.

I paddle all the way out to the other end of the lake and back. It's surprisingly quick with no wind—one of the best hours of my life. I remember my grandmother being so excited about her trip to Lake Louise, and I wonder if she can see me.

When I get back, Doug and Teri are waiting with Sonny, who they fetched from the van. Little Sonny sees his mommy in the kayak and dances with happy paws. The closer I get, the bigger his clown smile. He's trying to figure out how to get in the kayak with me because he is always my kayaking partner and he wants to go, but Doug holds him back. Adorable boy.

Moraine Lake

After lunch, we hike another ass-busting hike at Moraine Lake.

Today has been a tough hike, big paddle, then another tough hike. I need sleep.

A FEW BREATHS FROM DEAD AND STILL NO PLAN

The three of us have about killed ourselves hiking. When I returned to the van last night, it felt like I was a few breaths from dead. *That* is a new level of exhaustion for me. But this morning? I'm ready for more, just like I am every morning.

We go to Calgary for our last day together in Canada. Doug and Teri treat me to the most delicious steak dinner. I'll take them to the airport tomorrow morning, then start heading back.

I'm sad. They just got here.

And good grief, what the hell is wrong with me? I need to start heading east in the morning but have zero clues as to my route. I am nonstop Google mapping, but I still don't know what I'm doing.

Cross back through Canada? What about Montana/South Dakota/Minnesota and the rest? Maybe I should head back down to Wyoming and stop in Denver to regroup? That's probably smartest, but I don't want to retrace steps.

This is not a footloose and fancy-free moment. I am paralyzed by indecision because I don't want to do that long haul. Just get me to North Carolina! But the Smokies are 34 hours away in a car, probably forty or forty-five in the van. Then I still have at least another dozen hours driving back to Florida, whenever I decide to head home.

I look at the map over and over. Choose a route! I keep shouting in my head. Pick!

But I can't. I don't know.

There is no plan.

LONG HAUL

I wake up today and realize there are 3,300 miles and more than fifty or sixty hours of driving between me and my street. That is so intimidating. I need a few days to recover, but I want to be east of the Mississippi River *now*. There is no time for dawdling. I want to get close to home. I'm going to suck it up and go.

Now.

When I left home, I'd planned to get to Canada, then drop back down to Colorado, rest, then cross over through Nebraska and Kansas. The first half of the drive back would be a do-over, and the rest would be flat Midwest. It wasn't calling me.

I wake up with a plan. My first decision is to forgo the shortest route—through Saskatchewan. Gas is much more expensive in Canada than in the US. I have to do the math because it's metric in Canada, but most of the time, gas in Canada costs about $1.50 more per gallon. That route won't be especially scenic, either.

I decide to do the cross-country route through Montana, South Dakota, Minnesota, Wisconsin, Illinois, Missouri, Tennessee, North Carolina, Georgia, and back to Florida.

That will also reconnect me with a lot of friends I'd love to see.

I drop Doug and Teri at the airport and, damn, that makes me sad.

We had such a thrilling week, and I can't believe it's already behind us. But it is.

But, in this van life, it's always a matter of moving on to the next stop. Goodbye, Doug and Teri. Hello, open road.

I drive all day to get to Billings, Montana and think about continuing on because it's so hot here. It feels too hot to stop and camp without power. What else is there to do but drive?

Right now, there is wheat on my left and wheat on my right. I am on quiet Montana backroads. This is its own kind of adventure.

But I have to stop. Driving 535 miles solo in a van is torture. Enough is enough. I'm not sharp. These open roads are so beautiful, but I'm not in the mood to dawdle. I'll go to the Badlands tomorrow, and hopefully get to Sioux City or Sioux Falls, then St. Louis later in the week, then onward.

670 MILES OF OPEN SPACE

Unfortunately, I'm in a rush, focusing on the 1,800 miles still between me and the mountains of North Carolina, where I want to hang for a couple of weeks. I can't help but savor what I'm looking at in this part of Montana, where there is open space and endless fields of green farmland.

It is a privilege to have time to drive this. I drive fast because of the thousands of miles in front of me, but I do want to savor this time because my mind is clear, the sky goes forever, and the clouds are dramatic. It's hay bales, horses, and cows for miles and miles. I am so far from any significant civilization.

I like driving these rolling hills and farmlands so much more than the mountains. They are soothing, comfortable, and safe.

I don't want to rush through this, yet I'm pushing hard because I am so far from the Smokies, where I want to be. I am looking forward to those mountains. They are closer to home—twelve hours from Dunedin—but the Smokies are my home turf. That will feel good.

I see a whole lot of motorcycles, which was a concern in my route planning because the famous Sturgis, South Dakota bike rally is going on. I drive past Sturgis and don't even stop to people-watch. I don't want any part of it. I did stop to visit Wall Drug in South Dakota because I remember going there with my family when I was a kid. It's a tourist trap with T-shirts and hats. I can buy a $1.99 Sturgis T-shirt there, but that is $1.98 too much. I'm still glad I stopped here because it reminds me of my mom and dad.

My next stop is Badlands National Park, which I remember from childhood as being phenomenal. I drive in, climb out of the van, take some pictures then go to two more overlooks. It's a desolate beauty, but it seems so small and colorless compared to the canyons I've explored so many times in Utah and Arizona. For me, it is hot and uninviting. I don't want to hike it. I don't want to stay.

I drive all the way to Sioux Falls, South Dakota today. That's more than 670 miles, counting my detour to the Badlands. I started at 6:15 a.m. and finished twelve hours later. EXHAUSTED.

I realize that exhaustion is a common theme. I'll sleep soon.

The Badlands

ALONE TIME

For someone who's been on a solo trip for two months, I've sure been with a lot of people. I'm finally getting my alone time, and I need it.

Every time I tell people I'm an introvert, I get this response: "You?

182

Yeah, right!" I've made my living as a speaker who stands in front of hundreds or thousands of people at a time, and I maintain a lot of friendships, so it may look like I choose to always be around people. The truth is, I recharge alone. That makes me an introvert.

It's complicated because, for most of my life, I was a true extrovert. If I was going to dinner with a friend, I'd invite eight other people and often have ten people at the table. I'd get 15 friends to meet at my house to go cycling on a Saturday morning. I never needed and rarely wanted alone time.

That changed when I became an author and speaker. I would have so many people lined up waiting for my autograph, and I always tried to connect with every one of them because I was so grateful for their support. By the time I got home, I didn't want to talk to *anybody*.

I grew to love and crave solitude.

Introversion and extroversion refer to how we recharge. I used to get my energy by being in big groups of people. Now I want quality conversations with only a few people at a time. I generally do not go to parties or big group dinners, but if I do, I leave after 90 minutes.

I like it this way! There is no crime in being a quiet person who is happy and content with solitude.

I have alone time every day while I'm vannin', but there sure has been a lot of human interaction, When I fantasized about my trip, I thought I might see ten or 15 people, but I now know it will wind up being more than 70 by the time I'm done.

That said, I am really loving this drive time because I'm finally recharging in silence.

It feels good to have time to think about the places I've been and the old friends I've seen. I'm processing how this is changing me and what I'll be like when I go home. I keep thinking about all those stars in Jasper and how small and big I am as a person in this universe. I'm praying. I'm enjoying my solitude and refueling for the rest of my life.

STUPID GOOGLE MAPS

Would I be where I am today without Google Maps? No. But I don't trust that SOB app.

That became clear the day after I left home when stupid Google Maps routed me through Pensacola then suddenly told me to get off the interstate and head in the opposite direction. I figured I must have missed a turnoff, so I did what it said. Three miles later, it told me to get off the highway, then go back the way I had been going in the first place. It made me go through all of that, just to get where I already was. What the hell?

I would like to report that as a one-off, but by now it's probably a 12-off or even a 15-off because it keeps happening. Stupid Google Maps sends me in the right direction, then the wrong direction, then on some roads that have nothing to do with anything. The only solution is switching to Apple Maps, which isn't as good as Google when it comes to traffic problems and detours. I read up on this before I left in the Google vs. Apple vs. Waze reviews, and Google always gets the best ratings.

But when it's bad, it is *bad*. Stupid Google Maps took me 11 miles off-course in Kalispell, Montana. It routed me way up into Minnesota instead of through Iowa like it was supposed to. It sent me in circles in Billings. It had no idea what to do with me in Albuquerque. Yet here I am, relying on it one more time.

I can't believe I complain about it because, despite its too-frequent nervous breakdowns, Google Maps sure beats doing it with a regular map.

RUNNING AWAY

I just did something epic! I got a motel room in a Radisson in Madison, Wisconsin. I am so punch-drunk tired that the fact that Radisson rhymes with Madison is entertaining. It's not even funny, but that's how tired I am.

I desperately need a bed with clean sheets and air conditioning, and I want to take at least two showers. Sonny needs to get out of the van, too. He walks into the room and immediately climbs under the covers, hiding his head. He doesn't move for hours, and his snoring is darling.

I get it.

We are so stinking tired, and we need this break.

I had a good nap, and now I'm pondering life.

I've been told you can't run away from your problems, but I did. There's a lot of new life out in this big world when you don't see the same people and have the same conversations. I love not worrying about mail or email. I truly love it when I am out of range and my phone can't ring or ding with the latest text notification. There's relief when I'm not doing the next thing on the to-do list for my house.

My world has become my dog, my van, and the big outdoors. My problems are here with me somewhere. I've just forgotten to pay attention to them, so it feels like I have no problems.

Some people proclaim themselves nomads, head out in RVs, and don't come back for years, if ever. I'm not cut out for that. I feel stress creeping in because time is running out, and every minute brings me a little closer to "reality." Thoughts like, "When I get back, will my yard be dead?" or "Will my truck start?" or "What is broken at my house?" have me starting to worry. What will I have to deal with when I get back? I fear my mail stack. It must be massive, even though I've been monitoring it with the help of the USPS sending me screenshots of what is being delivered.

How much time am I going to spend fixing what fell apart in my absence? What kinds of bills have come that I didn't spot?

See? Reality is taunting me, and I'm trying to beat it back down.

I make the mistake of looking at LinkedIn. I see posts about productivity, leadership, blah, blah, blah, YUCK. I am so far out of that realm now and am in the most mentally healthy place I have ever been. Believe me, I understand all that. It's how I made my living. I was passionate about it. But right now, I cringe when I see the intensity of those posts.

The self-promotion and "humble bragging" have always made my stomach churn and, even when I needed to do it, I didn't do it well. At this point, I want no part of it.

Do I have to start paying attention to all of that ick again once I get home?

I am sick of that mindset. It has nothing to do with who I want to be from here on out.

I don't want reentry to be stressful, and I don't want to be sad that the adventure is over. I want to go back to eating popcorn in bed and falling asleep, cooled by central air conditioning, while watching travelers on YouTube on my big-screen TV.

But for now, I just stretch out on this king bed at the Radisson in Madison.

THE SMUGGLER

In other news…

I inadvertently became involved in an immigrant smuggling operation at the Canadian border four days ago. I stopped to let Sonny take a potty break and ended up accidentally transporting five undocumented Canadian flies into the US.

If only we'd built that wall! I try and try to get them to leave the van, but those pesky flies will not! I try shooing, slapping, and begging them to go. I open the windows, but they will not leave. I have now given up and refer to them as "the Canadians." I'm in Illinois, and the Canadians are still my stowaways. They are harmless to me, but I think they have procreated and their "anchor baby" flies might qualify for education and benefits. This is my argument for border security.

Clearly, I am still loopy, need another hotel room, and book one near Chicago.

I need a very, very long nap.

SO RICH

I am trying to get to Nashville and am sitting on the interstate, stuck. Traffic isn't moving, but I'm fine. I'm in no rush, which is good because the Waze app says we'll be sitting here for more than an hour. Other drivers act like this is the worst thing that ever happened. The honking! People are yelling out their windows—at whom? What good do honking and yelling do when the cause of the problem is several miles in front of us?

I could offer great Zen perspective on this, but the truth is that this situation is much easier for those of us who have a means of going to the bathroom while being stuck in traffic.

Instead of honking or driving in the emergency lane like others are doing, I'm going to think about how lucky I am to be here.

I once did a cycling trip through North Florida that bored me to death. Evenly spaced rows of longleaf pine trees to the left of us, evenly spaced rows of longleaf pine trees to the right. Every day. There were some hills, some flats, but all I saw were tall longleaf pine trees that bored the hell out of me on 60-, 70-, 80-mile cycling days.

I thought I would lose my mind.

I passed an older woman on her bike—definitely in her late 70s or 80s—and vented, "The scenery on this trip is boring me to death!"

She looked at me and said, "Well, I'm having a GREAT time!"

BOOM.

I will never forget that sage woman or what she taught me.

I was miserable, and she was delighted, yet both of us were riding on the same road and looking at the same scenery. I was embarrassed by my negativity.

I know how fortunate I have been to run away from home like this, so I don't care about the traffic. I also don't have to be anywhere at any specific time.

I was thinking about a woman I met last month in the shower line at the Molas Lake Campground in Colorado. She was a social worker who was off for two weeks of vacation with her kids, staying down the road on free public lands. She was so effusive as she described her vacation with her family, all sharing such precious time. We talked about what it means to be rich in life.

When you always want more, you never realize or fully appreciate what you have.

I feel so wealthy right now, yet I will be staying in a van in a hotel parking lot tonight. I have everything I need.

This all makes me think of the wealthiest man I ever knew.

Several years ago, I was a writing coach for a very rich man who made his fortune during the dot.com era. He had millions in the bank, yet he was the saddest, loneliest man I have ever known.

We were at a conference, working on his book in a hotel suite. The housekeeper came in, and my client said, "I don't need service today, but this is for you," handing her a fifty.

"Thank you so much!" she said and smiled broadly. "I take all of these tips and give them to my church." I saw a joy in her eyes that I had never seen in his. Peace. Fulfillment.

On paper, the housekeeper had nothing. But in her heart, she had everything. On paper, the multimillionaire had everything, but I knew him well and knew that in his heart, he had nothing.

He had success, acclaim, and financial reward—none of which brought him joy. He had six homes that he proclaimed to be "architectural masterpieces," but none of them made him happy. The beautiful girlfriend—who took his money but rarely spent time with him—didn't make him happy, either. Throughout the years, I watched him slowly destroy himself with alcohol. When he was 62, he drank so much that he tumbled down to the bottom of the stairs of his mansion, suffering a severe head injury that left him paralyzed. He is still in physical therapy. He can't manage a home. The money-grubbing girlfriend vanished after his fall.

He can now live independently in an apartment, but he walks with a walker. Such a sad, sad man. He had everything, but it was nothing.

I think we all have the same amount of happiness available to us regardless of how much money we have—as long as our survival and safety are assured.

Happiness is free. You have to open yourself to it. When you do, you find freedom—whether you are sleeping in a Four Seasons or its parking lot.

WRECK

Not even two miles from my friend Jae's house, I stop to check a map because my GPS is out. I stop in the empty parking lot of a tiny rural post office, figure out where I need to go, then start rolling again.

Tap!

Not BAM! Not BOOM! Not THUD!

It's a tap. I barely hear it, but I hear it. A Kia Sorento appears from God-knows-where, and I don't see it has moved in front of me. I see what I need on the map and mindlessly roll forward, suddenly hearing the tiniest "tap." Huh? I wonder what the noise is and then see the Sorento. A woman emerges, angry. I tapped her car at a whopping two mph. I did it, but for some reason, I'm mad at her.

The only damage I see is the reflector on the right side has been pushed in. It looks like a $50 repair, max, but I don't want it to go to the insurance company because I switched companies six months ago, and I already got that speeding ticket before I left home.

You can't even see it. The reflector pushed in by the tiniest bit. That is $1,300 in damage?

I offer her $500 cash, but she doesn't want it and tells me to stay put because she's calling the cops. For a tap on the bumper.

It was MY fault, but for some reason, I am mad at HER. She didn't do anything wrong.

We wait for almost an hour before the trooper comes. He's wonderful and tells her that we should work this minor accident out ourselves because her insurance premium will also go up. He writes a report, doesn't cite either of us, and finally, I am able to leave.

I am rattled.

And tired.

I have driven too far for too long.

ZAPPED

I am home! Not really.

Yup, my right rear wheel was hanging in mid-air off the side of the road.

But I am overjoyed when I pull into Deep Creek Campground in Smoky Mountain National Park in North Carolina because I come here every couple of years and, compared to where I have been, it feels like home, and I am delighted.

Sorting it out at Deep Creek

A very goofy intern park ranger points right and tells me to head that way to find my campsite. I do what he says, but I realize his directions are bad because I'm driving into a maintenance area with little room for me to turn around. I make a sharp turn to get back on the main road, but I miscalculate. Dammit! My right rear tire goes right off the side. And I mean *off*, because there is no shoulder, and I am stuck. The tire hangs in the air and, as hard as I try, I can't make the van pull itself back up onto the road. I carefully exit out the left side door and now see how precarious the situation is: The axle appears crooked and ready to break right off.

Good grief.

I carefully coax Sonny to come out my door, scared that movement will throw my van down the side of the road. Thankfully, it doesn't.

I walk to the ranger station, and he won't call a supervisor or a maintenance person who could easily pull the van up with a strap on a hitch.

"I'll let you use my phone to call a tow truck," he offers.

Ugh.

AAA says the tow truck is based in Silva—90 minutes away. Oh joy.

Two minutes have passed, and my phone rings. It's the tow truck driver.

"I happen to be in Bryson City," he says. "I'll be there in seven minutes."

He arrives in five, hooks my van up, and in one minute, all is right with the world again. What felt like a disaster turns out to be no big deal.

But I have to look at what's going on here. I am spent. I've been feeling it for weeks and thought those two hotel rooms would help me recover, but I am beyond worn out. I knew I was exhausted, but not so bad that I'd be making mistakes like this.

I hate to say it, but this has to be part of aging. I used to be all go, go, go. I'm learning that I now need to go, rest, go, rest, go and rest. I don't like the notion, but I'm going to lean into it so I will positively experience moments like what I am doing right now, enjoying quiet time in my hammock out in the woods. This is heaven. I need to do this more.

I don't trust my driving right now. I'm supposed to go to Jenny and Pat's tomorrow for two days and then to Lake Jocassee and Hiawassee and Tallulah Falls. I am not going to be home until around Labor Day in a couple of weeks.

I need to recover if I'm going to pull that off, but do I really need to keep traveling if I'm so worn out? I did the most amazing backpacking trip to Europe with three of my friends when I was 26. They each had three weeks. I had a little over four. We did the Eurail thing, traipsed through Europe with our backpacks, had the best time ever, and then said goodbye in Paris. I was heading to London for a week in the UK by myself.

This was before the Chunnel opened, so I went to Ostend, Belgium to spend the night before taking a hovercraft across the English Channel. I got myself a cozy, warm room at an inn—the first space I'd had to myself in all those weeks of youth hostels. I remember how I went into a sleep coma for 12 hours that night.

I woke up, went to England, and traveled around London and the surrounds. I saw the queen and Princess Anne, but other than that, the end part of my trip sucked. I was still traveling because I had time. But the trip really ended for me the minute my friends left. I was just going through the motions, trying to get through that ten days so I could get on the plane and go home.

It feels like that's what is going on now. By the time I left Canada, I'd experienced the best eight weeks of my life. Canada was definitely the high point of my trip and, yes, my plan has always been to head to North Carolina to enjoy the Smoky Mountains, which my soul loves. But I am in these mountains almost every year. This time, the Smokies are an add-on to what has been a perfect trip. It feels like forcing myself to tour London because I still had vacation time. Do I need to do this?

By the time I got here, I was wiped out. I needed to go comatose in a homey room in an inn like I'd found in Ostend, Belgium. But I kept moving every day. One night here, one night there, one night here, one night there. Even if I got a good night's sleep, I kept driving too many miles while pushing toward North Carolina.

Now that I'm here, I wonder what I'm trying to accomplish by staying.

I am depleted. The tiny accident yesterday and the incident with my wheel leaving the road today were really two big episodes of nothing because there was no significant damage and nobody was hurt. But in my exhausted mind, they still feel like huge incidents.

Imagine how bad it could have been!

I should never have driven 2,500 miles in a week by myself. Some people can do it. I can't. I was so drained after Canada, and I needed a good, long break. Instead of taking one, I focused on the miles in front of me.

More quality time with friends

I decided to suck it up and just go. In Montana, I felt carefree as I drove through endless miles of farmlands. Even in South Dakota, I felt strong. I didn't notice how my focus wasn't sharp and my energy was zapped. Never again will I do more than 1,200 miles in a week if I am the only driver.

If this sounds like a lot of complaining and whining, "I'm so tiiii-ired! Waaaah!"—it's not! Yeah, I'm beat. I don't like that. But I am now pulled because I get to go home to a place that I *love*. Home! It's starting to call me. That is not a bad thing at all! I look forward to sleeping in my bed, kissing my cats, and getting my favorite kayak out on the big water for sunrise and sunset.

I am trying to rally. But I am also starting to joyfully fantasize about home.

There's no place like home. There's no place like home. There's no place like home.

I click my heels together, but I still have 603 miles between me and my bed. That's really not all that far away…

AUNT OLD LADY

I decided to forgive Mason Burgess for what he did to me two years ago.

He's the son of Jenny and Pat Burgess, dear friends since they were newlyweds renting one of my houses. They left Florida, moved to North Carolina, and are incredible parents to Mason and his brother Miles, the two best kids ever, except for one thing: The boys call me "old lady."

This started a couple of summers ago after we'd all spent the day on a lake in North Carolina. As they were leaving, Mason shouted out the window, "Goodbye, old ladies!" to my friend and me.

Our mouths were agape as they drove off, and I finally shouted back, "It's Aunt Old Lady to you!" I swore I would never forgive them, but here I am in North Carolina at Jenny and Pat's mountain cabin and, well, I am a sucker for those rascals.

Sonny and I head out for a paddle in NC

Jenny takes a picture of me loving on the boys, and my two-toned hair with the scary gray roots helps me to see why they call me "old lady." Going gray has been a hideous, demoralizing experience. It is not going well for me on the exterior, which makes me vulnerable on the interior. In an effort to bolster my self-esteem in this terrible circumstance, I bribe the boys $10 each if they can go 24 hours without calling me "old lady."

As soon as I pay up, Mason says it again.

I have *got* to do something about this hair.

DONE

I am debating between kayaking the mountain lake where I am camping or heading up to Highlands, N.C. and hiking to scenic waterfalls.

I don't feel like doing any of it.

Is this it? Is it time to go home?

I know I'm done.

Done, done, done.

I am DONE.

There. I said it.

I am ready to figure out who I am when I'm not in this little van. I have ten more days of primo, impossible-to-get reservations to stay right on the water on Lake Chatuge in Georgia and Lake Jocassee in South Carolina.

Poof! I just canceled everything.

What relief!

I'm going home! I'm going home! I'm going home!

This doesn't have anything to do with the two little accidents. Well, of course it does. But also, I want to go home. I miss my home, I want to kiss my cats, I miss my friends. Pete Foley keeps posting pictures of Florida sunsets over the Gulf, and it makes me want to be back there and in my skin.

Besides.

The estimates from two body shops for that "accident" where I ever-so-lightly tapped the woman's Kia will cost me between $1,287 and $1,332.

That fender bender and the other incident were so small, yet so big in my mind because of my exhaustion. I have seen many cars on the side of the road that have been in disastrous accidents. Some were fatalities. But I am fine! I'm so blessed and protected. But I am exhausted, and those two little problems on the road are a sign that I need a time-out before something big happens.

With zero fanfare, I start the van and leave the campground, heading toward Georgia.

I am going *home*. Home! Joy!

I have seen 73 people in two months. After I see my friend Ed tomorrow, it'll be 74. That many intense social interactions is a lot for an introvert like me. I need to go home and not talk to anybody for a while.

I am proud of myself. I did not delay my dream for someday. I did it now while I'm healthy and still feel young. Look at what I just did! I did it! I didn't wait—I did what I've wanted to do for years. This story has the best beginning, middle, and end. After I get a little bit of rest, I get to start a new story. I am ready to figure out who I am when I'm not in this van, but everything that happened in this van will embolden who that person is forever forward.

I head right to Tallulah Gorge State Park where my friends Peggy and George Schott happen to be camping. I cry when I see Peggy, a close friend from home. I need to be held, and she holds me tight.

With Peggy, George and Stroodle

It's everything I need, and in this moment, I apparently need a lot.

Sonny is also delighted to see Peggy's poodle, Stroodle. And, of course, we all love George.

We had such a nice dinner together, and then I came to my van for quiet time. I just looked at my list of the things I thought I would miss about home. When I checked it a month ago, I only missed four things: my loved ones, my cats, my washer/dryer, and my daily visits to the Y.

Now I miss every single thing on my list. I am getting so excited because it won't be long before I get my life back and come back to everything on the list:

1. My loved ones
2. My cats
3. My home
4. Having a bathroom right next to my bed that I can use whenever I want, day or night
5. The bidet seat in the bathroom
6. Hot showers whenever I want them
7. The ice-maker in my fridge
8. Jumping on the golf cart to go to town
9. Taking the ferry to Clearwater Beach
10. Cycling the Pinellas Trail
11. My washer and dryer
12. Hammock Park
13. Great neighbors
14. My full-size, super-duper Ninja Foodi (far superior to the tiny Instant Pot I brought with me)
15. Kayaking the best place to kayak in the whole world, which is five minutes from my house
16. Sunrise paddles
17. Sunset paddles
18. Full moonset paddles
19. The enormous televisions in my living room and bedroom
20. Easy Wi-Fi
21. Jumping in my truck to go somewhere
22. Swimming at the Y
23. My microwave
24. Dr. Julia Jenkins
25. Always bumping into people I know
26. Downtown Dunedin
27. Costco, Sam's, and BJ's
28. Paddling the Weeki Wachee River

29. Tubing Florida rivers in the summer
30. Sunset swims with Nancy

ONE LAST STOP

Almost everything for the last nine and a half weeks has been unplanned, but I always knew my last stop, to the Dames Ferry campground in Juliette, Georgia, would be my last stop. This is where my 85-year-old friend, Ed, is the camp host.

With Ed, who is family to me. We had lunch at the real Whistle Stop Cafe, where the classic, Fried Green Tomatoes, was filmed.

Ed taught me almost everything I know about RVs. He's mentored me through a pop-up, travel trailer, and now, the van.

He's family. His wife, Martha, was a close friend before she passed two years ago. Ed couldn't stand the loneliness and went back to hosting in campgrounds. His assignment is six hours and thirteen minutes from my home, so it's a perfect last stop.

He took me to the nearby Whistle Stop Café, where *Fried Green Tomatoes* was filmed. I ordered fried chicken livers—proof that, yes! I am back in the South.

I pray for a safe, easy drive home. I hope my landing is soft. I hope I won't melt when confronted with the first real heat I have experienced since June 16. I hope I don't get in a funk because it's over. I have loved this adventure, and I would cry about it being over except I'm too tired to cry and too happy about seeing my cats. I remember my malaise after returning from the first time I went to Europe. The new, improved me came back to the same old shit, and that was depressing.

But I learned then how to deal with it: All I had to do was plan another trip.

HOMEWARD BOUND

I wake up at 2 a.m., too excited and nervous to sleep. "Too early to leave," I keep telling myself, but at 3:40 a.m., I know it's hopeless, so I climb out of bed, walk Sonny, then drive off.

I can sleep later, I figure, in my own bed.

I have learned that "there is no plan" is a mighty good plan.

Twenty minutes into my drive, Google Maps tells me to turn around. I ignore the prompt because Google has messed up so many times. *What does stupid Google Maps know?* I ask myself as I keep going (in the wrong direction). When I most want to be heading south, I finally realize I am going north.

Yup. A 16-mile error at 4:27 in the morning when all I want to do is get home.

I know the level of my exhaustion. "Dear God, please get us home safely," I pray again.

Crossing the Florida border brings me to tears. I say a prayer and sing my favorite hymn from childhood. It comes straight out of my heart.

Then, I feel it.

"We're home!" I say to Sonny. "We're home! We're home! We're home!"

Waaaaaahooooo! We are in Florida.

I sing "City of New Orleans" as loud as I can sing along with Willie Nelson. I am especially off-key, but I'm so happy and think I sound fabulous. Every mile marker means I am one mile closer.

But I have conflicting feelings: ecstatic and disappointed all at once. Those nine and a half weeks felt like a lifetime, but they passed in a heartbeat.

I moved to Florida when I was 15 and, except for the eight-year intermission when I lived in Colorado, it's been my home. Florida is where I am my most comfortable self. I just saw a road sign telling me how far I am from Ocala, Tampa, and Miami. Seeing the word "Tampa" on a sign makes me tear up. This is crazy! Getting emotional over a road sign?

As screwed up as my state seems to other people, screwy Florida is my home.

I pass Gainesville. Closer, closer, closer to Dunedin. So glad to get home, so sad for the adventure to end. Glad, sad, glad, sad. I am stronger, happier, and so much younger than when I left. I learned so much about life. Almost everything went smoothly. I felt safe almost 100 percent of the time.

I can't wait to see my house. Julie swears it's still right where I left it, just as I left it. Two miles from home, Sonny stands on his couch. He knows. He sure does. He sticks his face between the front seats and nudges my elbow when we are on our street.

After nine and a half weeks of excitement and exhaustion, we are one minute from being home safe.

"Sonny! Are you ready, boy? Are you ready to go home? We did it, little boy! We did it." The recorder catches my words and the tears that come with them as we close in on the driveway. One more block to go, after 9,852 miles.

And there it is. Home. My home. I am home.

My friend Lisa is waiting for us out front, which makes me blubber even more.

There's no place like home, there's no place like home, there's *no* place like home.

Sonny Germer is the happiest he has ever been. I think he accepted he would be spending the rest of his life stuck in a little van.

And now, he sees his home. Little Man starts whimpering.

"We're home, Sonny! We're home! We're home, baby! We did it!" I cry.

He lets out a rare howl.

I open the side door, and Sonny flies out of the van, his tail wagging, wagging, wagging as he races to the front door. He runs through his house, from room to room, wearing his biggest goofy clown smile. He makes sure everything is still where it used to be, then runs to the sliding glass doors so he can run into his backyard. Sonny bolts out, then stops abruptly at the pool's edge to check what "the snake" is doing. This cracks me up. "The snake" is the pool vacuum. Sonny has to check the snake, like he does every time he goes out, before running out the doggie door to the yard where his much-missed Jolly Ball is still waiting for him.

Oh, happy day! Has any dog ever been so happy?

When I take him over to Hammock Park, he pees at least 450 times there and throughout the neighborhood to ensure every dog in Dunedin knows that Sonny Germer is back and still boss.

Little Man is home.

I've been home a few hours now and take a long look at myself in my bathroom mirror. The woman I see bears no resemblance to the young, empowered woman I am on the inside. I suddenly see my gray hair for what it is: an ugly mess.

I'd hoped that, by not coloring my hair, I'd come home with perfect white, flowing Emmylou Harris hair. What I got was old lady scrub. I kept deluding myself into thinking I was only days away from turning the corner and seeing how beautiful my natural hair really was. But today, I see the truth.

I open a box of Nice'n Easy No. 6, mix and apply the color, wait, rinse it out in the shower, then go back to the mirror.

Here stands Fawn Germer. The brown-haired Fawn.

I brush and dry it, then look at myself over and over again because I am so shocked at how a $9 box of hair dye can make me feel and be so much younger. If I ever doubt my desire to color my hair, I will look at the

The joy of brown hair!

pictures I took with the Burgess boys on my lap when I visited them in North Carolina. I looked like a grandma. Or a grandma's grandma.

It's sad that so much of our self-esteem comes from our looks because, as we age, so much is out of our control. At this point, I don't battle my wrinkles with Botox or surgery because that is fruitless. I've damaged my skin by spending my life in the sun. But I do have options when it comes to my hair.

I am getting older, but I don't have to surrender to being old.

. . .

The Last Facebook Post from the Trip

I'm home. I started crying when I crossed the Florida state line and blubbering when I pulled up in front of my house and Lisa Devereaux was there.

I am incredibly proud. I confronted my fears about safety (I never did opt for packing a gun) and never once felt alone because of my little rock star pit bull, Sonny Germer, the Mountain Kangaroo.

I drove 9,848.7 miles, averaged 17.1 miles to the gallon, and spent $2,189 on gas. I stayed in beds at friends' homes four nights but preferred sleeping in my dark, cozy van with Little Man. I was in the van for 60 nights. After the long haul out of Calgary, I booked a hotel room.

One thing I never shared with you for fear of jinxing my good luck was that it rained less than one hour in 9½ weeks. I think there were some evening storms, but I slept so hard that I never noticed.

None of this would have happened without Jane Nottenburg, who took in my cats and told me to go have the adventure of a lifetime. Her kindness has changed how I will see every day for the rest of my life. Julie Hipp checked my house every week and made sure where I was every day. She also surprised me with chicken and rice (my favorite!) today. I also have to mention Wendy Kissinger, who taught me about van life and even picked up my folding kayak for me in St. Augustine from a woman who posted it on Facebook Marketplace.

I saw 74 friends, many of whom I hadn't seen in decades. I wasn't planning to see so many people, but it was such a powerful experience. It felt like I was tying all the pieces of my life together. Thank you everybody for all of your kindness.

And you all, my Facebook family. You were my cheerleaders. I loved sharing my stories and photos with you. I was so touched by your encouraging comments. I have a book in my head. I need to get it out of me. And, oh — think of the keynote!

What was my favorite moment of the trip? When I camped on a woman's 14,000-acre farm in Three Forks, Montana. Just me and my boy, spellbound by the most beautiful sunset that I have ever seen. I will look at those photos over and over again.

I've lost seven friends in the last few months, from age 58 to 70. None of them were planning on dying young. The message is so clear: Live NOW. See your

*loved ones NOW. Travel NOW. Your time is priceless. If you get a block of
time for an adventure, USE IT! I'd rather spend 9½ weeks sleeping in a van
than blow my travel budget on one or two weeks in a nice hotel. If you have to
go it alone, DO IT! You might find out that your greatest relationship is with
yourself, and that you are stronger than you ever imagined.*

*Most important: A great dog is mandatory in this life. I got mine for 10 bucks
at animal control. You could offer me $10 million for him, but I wouldn't take
it. No way.*

I love you all. It's great to be home.

For now.

The post received 574 likes and got 272 comments from people who
keep saying how they had looked forward to my daily posts, how they
were traveling with me, and how inspiring my trip was for them.

Not sure what the big deal is. All I did was take my dog on a very
long drive. But I decided not to wait. That's the big thing. There is no
time to wait.

HOME AGAIN

Sonny needs a bath, but I don't want to wash the scent of our adventure off of him. I wonder if he knows that *he* is the reason my experience was so meaningful or that my life is so full. Am I supposed to
love a dog this much? Because that's scary.

There were so many reasons not to leave home. I was afraid to do it
alone. I feared for my safety. I was worried it would cost too much
money. I feared I would break down and not know what to do. I was
afraid my knee would give out, or I'd fall while hiking the backcountry
and nobody would find me.

Then there was the reason I *had* to leave home.

I was stuck.

I was a middle-aged woman who realized I wasn't middle-aged
anymore. That didn't feel good. I never sensed much of an age shift
between 40, 45, 50, and 55. Sixty *sounded* different, but I was in great
shape and was proud that I felt as young as I had at 40. Something
changed inside of me at 62. I was still working out *hard*—about three

hours a day—but I looked in the mirror and saw somebody who could no longer pretend she was super-cool, young-acting, and maybe a little bit middle-aged. I really am getting older. I am a professional speaker in an industry where looks and youth count. That old cliché, "age is just a number," is meaningful until people start dismissing you, your friends start dying, and your body starts having issues.

Then age becomes something you have to outfox. I want longevity, but only if it's good longevity, so I had to learn how to fight for my life.

Who was I going to be in this next installment of my wild and wonderful life?

The wonder of my pivot to the road is it gave me a chance to do what I love most: write. I've been a writer since the beginning, and this is what will carry me to the finish.

It seemed like leaving for so long to go so far by myself would be a big, scary experience. It wasn't that at all. It woke me up. It connected me to people I didn't even know I missed.

I realize now that connection on Facebook is very different from what happens when I'm sitting with friends, catching up, reminiscing, and sharing dreams for the future. In person, there is no hiding our wrinkles or the ten or 20 pounds we have gained or lost. What a luxury to share what went right or wrong in life. It helped me understand my life better.

But also, it's so damn fun to see everybody.

I was free and alive out there doing endless hours of driving, feeling happy to be somewhere, anywhere, or nowhere. The negative thoughts that had made me feel insecure and doubt myself vanished. As did the anxiety that had hit me because of the chaos that defines our politics and our world. I discovered a quiet calm that I'd never slowed down long enough to experience. All I had to do was count some dandelions on a mountaintop or go for a long drive.

I spent a lot of time being mindful by doing things that were often mindless.

Michelle told me what it's like being a mom with kids in the swimming pool. The edges of the pool are where they go for safety and security. Out in the middle, they play, splash, do flips, wear themselves out, and when they start to struggle and run out of breath, they go to the side of the pool to catch their breath and feel safe. Then they head right back out there to continue in their escapades. They need that one-minute reminder of their safe spot.

And that is why I am home. I have my home, my town, my friends, my park, my Y, the Gulf of Mexico.

I need a minute in my safe spot. I need to catch my breath.

And then I will head back out to play again.

I do think a trip around Florida would be great. Maybe go kayaking in a different location every day. Wouldn't that be fun? Do some of the rivers, hit the Panhandle, get my friends Malea and Teresa to do some camping in North Florida with me. Kayak Kings Landing. Go down to Palm Beach, Biscayne National Park, the Keys. That sounds pretty cool. Two weeks. Yeah, two weeks. That would be a blast.

Or maybe I'll go stay at a bunch of Florida farms on Harvest Host. That farm in Montana was so incredible. I bet ours are, too.

Michelle told me that if I won a billion dollars in the Powerball, I'd still live the same way I live now—but I would never think about money. That's probably true. I'd get a handyman on retainer and a housekeeper who comes every other day, and I'd get a bigger van with a bathroom and a generator. Maybe another house in Colorado or North Carolina—or both—but they wouldn't be big. If I don't get all or any of that, I'm still good. I'm free.

I have my van.

Who gets to be this lucky? I have what I need. It's more than enough.

My heart broke over and over again as I processed so many friends dying or becoming ill this year. The lesson I will carry with me every day is: *Don't wait. Don't wait. Don't wait.* Everything is uncertain, and the older we get, the faster it seems that time is running out. Well, time *is* running out.

I can't wait. None of us can.

I've long said that I could die tomorrow and everybody would know that I lived a great life and left with no unfinished business. I want to die with my hiking boots on, and I don't want to linger at the end.

But there is a complication now. I used to feel that I'd done enough to add up to a full, complete, happy life. But after my awakening in that little van with my magical dog, I realize I'm just getting started.

I don't want to go.

I want to be free again, driving open roads to some destination or no destination. It doesn't matter. I want the freedom.

So I pray that God gives me more.

I want to live and live and live and live.

ACKNOWLEDGMENTS

I was able to live this dream because Jane Nottenburg took in my cats and Julie Hipp checked on my home. I am so unbelievably grateful.

To my A-team, alphabetical: Lisa Alfe, Jean Berkompas, Beverly Billings, Kathy Bowers, Dan Bracewell, Shane Bracewell, Jayne Bray, Michelle Brigman, Kathy Carlson, Kathy Casey, Cindy Cole, Tracie Cone, Lisa Devereaux, Joyce Duarte, Susan Edwards, Kim Feil, Rob Frierson, Tanya Frierson, Jim Germer, Jeannine Germer, Malea Guiriba, Monica Kok, Happy Jordan, Nancy June, Dana Kuehn, Donna Larson, "Big Daddy" John Larson, Donna Law, Teresa Lawrence, Sarah MacDonald, John MacDonald, Rosemary O'Hara, Tom O'Hara, Tina Proctor, Susan Reynolds, Geoff Roth, Doug Swift, Teri Swift, Joan Toth, Susan Tripp, Emilia Vergara, Rebecca Whitley, Austin Zakari, Patri Zayas. Also, to my late mother and father, who guide me every day.

To my friends who died so unbelievably young: I promise I will live every moment in honor of you. Special hearts to Linda Lindsay, Jeanne Elliott, Wendy Barmore, Nancy Carney, Patty Lemke, Eva Krzewinski, Kurt Winselmann, and Lori Heitanen. Sadly, I now have to add my close friend Jill Cobb to this too-long list. I wrote here about her telling me she had cancer. Less than a year later, she is gone and I am crushed.

To Dr. Julia Jenkins, my badass primary care doc, who keeps me healthy and strong. To Dr. Leana Oppenheim, the neurologist who gave me the all-clear on my memory issue.

To Lois Creamer and Sam Horn, two dear friends and mentors. To Diane King, who read this long before it was ready to be read. And to Patty Ivey who made me realize why I had to move forward with it.

To Susan Edwards, my editor, coach, protector, and friend. This book exists because of Susan. My life is so much richer with her in it.

To rockstar editor Carolyn DiPaolo who has such perspective with words and life, and did an amazing first read, To my copy editor Lori Draft who's saved me from typos and style errors for more than a decade.

To the many friends I saw along the way. Reconnecting was a golden moment in my life. Thank you for the driveways, the food, and most of all, for making such an effort to get together and get caught up. I love you: Pete Foley, Karin Thrift, Michelle Brigman, Ajax Daugherty, Barbara Daugherty, Marie Quintana, Jill Shoush, Cathy Martindale, Dave Wohlfarth, Kyla Thompson, Roger Thompson, Amy McClintock, Cindiman Pinneke, Dean Krakel, Tara Finnegan, Greg Wright, Brian Campbell, Cheryl Campbell, Diane King, Scott Wesley, Betsy Cannon, Laurie Cannon, Tina Proctor, Dennis Grogan, Shelley Gonzalez, Mike Wilson, Becky Cantwell, Debby Frazier, Karen Krizman, Steve Krizman, Chris Broderick, Mary Gay Broderick, Ann Meadows, Miriam Reed, Kathy Bowers, Joe Moran, Rachel Moran, Janet Reeves, Chip Reeves, Linda McConnell, Richard Sharkey, Caroline Little, Jim Little, Micki Frederikson, John Frederikson, Patri Zayas, Christine Tutty Johnson, Eamonn Johnson, Annilise Johnson, Eirnin Johnson, Jennifer Shryock, Kent Meireis, Geri Meireis, Doug Swift, Teri Swift, Erin Johansen, Paul Saltzman, Carolyn Yousse, Lois Creamer, Dick Creamer, Jeff Truesdell, Jae Jackson, Patrick Burgess, Jenny Burgess, Mason Burgess, Myles Burgess, Peggy Schott, George Schott, and Ed Lemasters.

Lucky, lucky me to be blessed with such friends.

ABOUT THE AUTHOR

Fawn Germer is the best-selling author of ten books and has been the motivational keynote speaker for nearly 100 Fortune 500 companies. Her first career, in journalism, led her to be a highly acclaimed investigative reporter with four nominations for the Pulitzer Prize. Her first book, rejected everywhere, was an Oprah book.

Enough of that.

Fawn is a kayaker, dog lover, hiker, cyclist, swimmer, camper, stargazer, sunrise lover, sunset addict, good friend, and a somewhat intro-verted, generally happy person who lives in Dunedin, Florida with her dog Sonny and two cats, Coconut and Teddy. She loves big water, blue skies, tall trees, classic rock (especially the Rolling Stones), and her big-screen TVs.

For coaching and speaking information, write info@fawnger mer.com, visit fawngermer.com, or call 727-467-0202.

OTHER TITLES BY FAWN GERMER:

Hard Won Wisdom, Perigee Books, 2001

Mustang Sallies, Perigee Books, 2004

Mermaid Mambo, Newhouse Books, 2007

The NEW Woman Rules, Network Books, 2007

Finding the UP in the Downturn, Newhouse Books, 2009

The Ah-Hah! Moment, Strauss Books, 2010

Pearls, Newhouse Books, 2012

Work-life Reset, Boulevard Books 2015

Coming Back!, St. Martin's Press, 2021

Made in United States
Orlando, FL
03 January 2025

56874225R00127